THE MOSAIC HANDBOOK FOR MICROSOFT WINDOWS
ADDENDUM

Installing Mosaic
Page 19

Typing **a:setup** from the DOS prompt launches Windows and the Mosaic Setup Program. You can also run the Mosaic Setup Program from within Windows. To do this:

1. In the Program Manager, select **Run** from the **File** menu.

2. Type **a:setup** and press **Return**.

The Mosaic Setup Program will automatically create a new program group and program item for Mosaic, so you should not have to do this yourself.

Specifying a Proxy Server
Pages 100 and 109

The EMOSAIC.INI file comes with the following section:

```
[Services]
Proxy_Server=
NNTP_Server=
```

You need to fill in the name of your proxy server using the following syntax:

```
http://proxy.server.name:portnumber/
```

For example:

```
Proxy_Server=http://fakeproxy.ora.com:80/
```

Also, depending on which TCP/IP stack you are using, you may have to change the underscore between the words "Proxy" and "Server" into a space. For example:

```
Proxy Server=http://fakeproxy.ora.com:80/
```

A proxy server can also be set in the **Preferences** dialog.

Stopping a Transfer

To stop Mosaic from transferring a document, press the **Escape** key.

Changing Your Home Page
Page 107

There is a syntax error in this section. The correct syntax is:

Home Page=URL

Printing Problems

There may be several reasons for printing problems. Often, it's a matter of not having enough RAM either in your computer or in your printer. Try printing the page without graphics; if that works, you probably need more memory. Version 2.0 of the software will deliver more robust printing, which may solve your printing problems.

Problems with PKUNZIP
Page 122

The version of PKUNZIP on the Colorado State server is buggy and out-of-date. A much better version exists at *ftp://ftp.ora.com/pub/pkunzip.exe.*

Problems with FTP

Some users have reported problems with accessing FTP servers via Enhanced Mosaic. If you are experiencing problems with FTP, you may have to use a dedicated FTP client or terminal program.

THE
MOSAIC
HANDBOOK

For Microsoft Windows

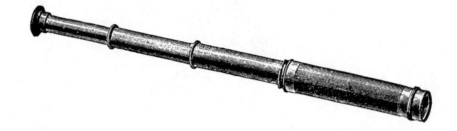

THE
MOSAIC
HANDBOOK

For Microsoft Windows

DALE DOUGHERTY & RICHARD KOMAN

O'REILLY & ASSOCIATES, INC.
103 MORRIS STREET, SUITE A
SEBASTOPOL, CA 95472
(800) 998-9938 • (707) 829-0515
EMAIL: *nuts@ora.com*

The Mosaic Handbook for Microsoft Windows
by Dale Dougherty and Richard Koman

Editor: Dale Dougherty

Production Editor: Clairemarie Fisher O'Leary

Printing History:

October 1994:   First Edition.

ISBN: 1-56592-094-5   [12/94]

TABLE OF CONTENTS

CHAPTER TWO
GETTING STARTED WITH MOSAIC _____ 17

CHAPTER THREE
EXPLORING THE WORLD WIDE WEB _____ 41

FIGURES

TABLES

FOREWORD

I always enjoy giving demos of Mosaic and showing people interesting places to go on the Internet. At tradeshows or in boardrooms, whether there's one person or many looking over my shoulder or watching it on a big screen, I watch to see when they "get" it. When do they really get the power of Mosaic? When do they really understand what the Internet makes possible? When do they realize that this is something they always wanted to do with a computer?

One thing I usually do when Mosaic appears on the screen is to distinguish between the Mosaic interface and the document that is displayed. I say, "When I use the scrollbar, which Mosaic provides, everything that moves is in the document window, where formatted documents containing text and graphics are displayed. The document itself contains any number of hypertext links, or connections to other documents anywhere on the Net. I move the mouse pointer over a link and click on it. Right away, Mosaic begins retrieving the document from a remote information server."

Then I stop and explain that the document I just retrieved came from Geneva, Switzerland. Usually, someone smiles. Next I get a document from a server in Australia and yet another from a university in Texas. At that point, someone usually asks a question, just to be sure. This gives me the chance to stop and emphasize to the audience that we are traveling great distances across the Internet. Sometimes there is a delay in making a long-distance connection, and then I have the opportunity to make the same point. But often enough the document pops up on the screen, just as if it were on my local system. "Did you see that?" I ask. "I just got that document from a World Wide Web server in Vancouver, B.C."

Mosaic makes it easy to navigate the Internet, and the connections that it makes are transparent to the user. I begin to worry that the audience might not grasp the power behind such a simple interface. So, I explain what the World Wide Web is.

While Mosaic manages the user interface and the display of documents—in other words, what is visible to the user—the World Wide Web (WWW) is invisible. The WWW is an information architecture, developed at CERN, a particle physics lab in Geneva, Switzerland. The WWW defines the components of a global information system and how they work together. I try to explain how clients like Mosaic are used to access information servers out on the network. How the clients and servers talk to each other is established by a WWW protocol specification known as HTTP (HyperText Transfer Protocol).

The World Wide Web specifications are public, and anyone can follow them to build a client; there is even code available that takes care of common functions. Indeed, that is how Mosaic was developed at the National Center for Supercomputing Applications (NCSA) at the University of Illinois. The virtue of public specifications is that from the outset, the World Wide Web recognized the need to have clients for all platforms. This was fully realized when NCSA came out with versions of Mosaic for the X Window System, Microsoft Windows, and the Macintosh.

As a graphical browser, Mosaic has managed to redefine what it means to be on the Internet. Instead of typing long command lines and having to remember a lot of arcane details, users can find the best the Net has to offer with a couple of mouse clicks. As if that isn't enough, when I show people that Mosaic can be used for multimedia, their reaction is one of disbelief, of seeing the future today. "Can you really find sound and video on the Net?" Yes, I answer, and although it may be impractical today for you to download digital sound bites or MPEG movie clips, the capability is there. The result can be stunning, and worth the wait. As the speed of network connections improve, so much more is possible.

The emergence of Mosaic and the WWW is the most exciting computing development in a decade, supplying the infrastructure needed to usher in the Age of Networked Information. Already, it is changing how people think and work, from elementary school children to CEOs. More and more people are discovering that they can move through the rich landscape of the Internet, find its wealth of resources, and contribute to its growth by becoming information publishers themselves.

It is also redefining what it means to be a publisher. With the *Global Network Navigator*, O'Reilly & Associates is exploring this new territory, and learning how to serve a new audience of online customers. Mosaic is also changing the way businesses and other organizations distribute information. Companies like Digital and Boeing, for instance, are setting up Web servers to distribute employee handbooks, sales sheets, and policies. Users are creating their own home pages and listing their hobbies or favorite places to visit on the Net.

All in all, the World Wide Web is becoming an incredible, enormous interconnected network of information, public and private, commercial and educational, free and for-pay. If you have an Internet connection, all you need is Mosaic to begin exploring these resources on your own.

Well, maybe, that's not all you need. Things are not as easy as they seem in a demo. Knowing where to go and what to do on your own can be a lot more challenging, especially given the size of the Internet. Learning how to navigate the Net and keeping up with all the new resources that are added every day is not easy. That's one reason we created *GNN*, so that you can find this information online and not have to spend your time gathering it. It is also why we developed *The Mosaic Handbook*. This book is more than a description of the Mosaic interface; it's a guide to navigating the Internet.

Dale Dougherty
Publisher, *GNN*

PREFACE

Welcome to Mosaic, the program that turns most folks' conception of the Internet on its ear. Forget about the Net being hard to use. Forget about command-line interfaces. Forget about UNIX commands.

You are about to enter the World Wide Web—a strange and fascinating land of hypertext, color graphics, digital video, interactive maps, and other cool stuff. Follow its strands and you'll wind a path through underground music archives, online newspapers and magazines, a warehouse of scientific knowledge, up-to-the-minute weather maps and traffic reports, interactive services, and so much more.

But Mosaic is more than just a Web browser. In fact, it's an integrated interface for the entire Internet. Most services on the Net—including Gopher, WAIS, FTP, newsgroups, and more—can be accessed through Mosaic.

How big is the Web? No one's really sure, since there's no central server registration point, but Matthew Gray, an MIT student who is the author of a program that travels the Internet seeking out new forms of Web life, sums it up pretty well: "Wow, it's big," he says.

But what exactly *is* the World Wide Web? It's a seemingly infinite system of servers on the Internet all tied together by hypertext links. Hypertext is a technology for linking collections of documents. On the Internet, these collections are distributed among a web of information servers. Using a mouse, you can click on a hypertext link in one document and retrieve the linked document from an information server out on the Internet. That server could be anywhere in the world.

The documents that you get can have a lot more than just text. Mosaic supports multimedia documents, and on the Web you can find graphics, video, audio, and other digital media.

The Best of the Net

What kind of information servers will you find on the Web? We'll cover that in some depth in this book, but to give you an idea of what's out there, here are some of the servers that in 1994 were named the "Best of the Net" by the *Global Network Navigator* (*GNN*), O'Reilly & Associates' online publications center and guide to Internet resources. In the images that accompany the descriptions of these servers, you'll see different documents displayed within the Mosaic interface. Mosaic displays documents within the area surrounded by the scroll bars.

International Teletimes

This general-interest magazine is published online from Vancouver, British Columbia, on a shareware model. According to its writer's guidelines, "Teletimes seeks to present informed opinion and observation drawn from the experience of living in a particular place." International Teletimes is a collaboration of many volunteers from around the world, but perhaps most notable is the fact that its editor-in-chief, Ian Wojtowicz, was 16 years old when he received the Best of the Net award.

New Zealand Information

Perhaps you are traveling to New Zealand, or teaching a class about it. A server at Carnegie-Mellon University will tell you more about New Zealand than you might want to know. Want to know about the climate, or locate Auckland on a map? Listen to a speech in the native Maori language? Want to know what a tuatara is? The most ancient of all living reptiles, and the sole survivor of the beak-heads family, the tuatara lives to be over 100 years old. What's more, while young the tuatara has a third eye. You'll also find out that the main difference between Marmite and Vegemite, two types of yeast extract, is that the latter is Australian and tastes awful.

U.S. Bureau of the Census

The self-proclaimed "Factfinder for the Nation," the Census Bureau has created a model server for government agencies to follow. In short, it organizes information so that citizens can make their own use of it. You can get financial data on state and local governments as well as schools. The Bureau's statistical briefs are PostScript documents describing poverty in the U.S., analyzing housing changes from 1981–1991, or profiling people of Asian and Pacific Island heritage in the American population. In the Census Bureau Art Gallery, there is a display of posters used to promote participation in the census.

Xerox PARC Map Viewer

From the famous research lab that gave birth to the technologies that would become the Apple Macintosh and Adobe PostScript (among others), here's one of the most interactive applications on the Net. MapViewer is an application that dynamically renders a map based on user input. Click on a region and MapViewer will zoom in on it. You can also use a geographic name server to locate a particular location by name. Typing in "San Jose, California," we find that it is the county seat, and had a population of 62,000 in 1980. Its latitude and longitude are also given, and we can click on this information to display a map of the U.S. and a map of Northern California showing where San Jose is.

The Geographic Name Server happens to be located at the University of Buffalo, but that's how the Net works—one computer connects to another, just as one person's work connects to what other people are doing. A map of the world that is created dynamically seems the best way to think of our own new world, where the boundaries of nations and the limits of individuals can be overcome by making so many different connections possible.

Those are just four of the thousands of servers on the Web, with new ones coming online every day. Of course, not all of them are absolutely riveting. Helping you find the ones that interest you is what this book is really all about.

"Wherever you go, there you are," a line from the movie *The Adventures of Buckaroo Bonzai Across the Eighth Dimension*, sort of sums up what Mosaic and the Web are all about. The Web is made for browsing, for following trains of thought, for taking interesting detours whenever they crop up. Mosaic users have a sense of the explorer about them, an excitement about discovering new information, a lust for links.

What This Book Is About

The Mosaic Handbook for Microsoft Windows is aimed at everyone who uses Mosaic—or who wants to use Mosaic—to access the Internet. Whether you're a rank beginner or an experienced Net-surfer who wants a guide to Web sites or help with customizing Mosaic, we think you'll get something out of this book.

Chapter 1, *The Wide World of Internet Services*, provides an overview and history of the Internet, including the development of the World Wide Web and Mosaic.

Chapter 2, *Getting Started with Mosaic*, describes how to begin using Enhanced NCSA Mosaic and covers the most important aspects of the Mosaic interface.

Chapter 3, *Exploring the World Wide Web*, covers how to navigate through the World Wide Web. It includes a tour of *GNN* and provides pointers to some of the more fascinating places on the Web.

Chapter 4, *Exploring Other Internet Services*, describes how to use Mosaic as a browser for Gopher, FTP, WAIS, and News.

Chapter 5, *Customizing Mosaic*, explains how to make changes in Mosaic's default behavior.

Chapter 6, *Using Mosaic for Multimedia*, gives the lowdown on using other programs to play audio, video, and other multimedia files.

Chapter 7, *Creating HTML Documents*, gives a tutorial in how to write your own Web documents.

Chapter 8, *Future Directions*, discusses future development of the Web. It introduces the new World Wide Web Organization (W3O), which is a development consortium founded by MIT and CERN.

Appendix A, *Mosaic Reference Guide*, describes the user functions available from Mosaic's menus.

Appendix B, *HTML Reference Guide*, describes the HTML tags used to create World Wide Web documents.

Enhanced NCSA Mosaic

The Mosaic Handbook for Microsoft Windows includes Enhanced NCSA Mosaic on two disks.

Enhanced NCSA Mosaic is based on the original Mosaic developed at the National Center for Supercomputing Applications (NCSA). However, it is not a public domain program, nor is it the same as the versions that can be downloaded from the Net.

Spyglass, Inc. was chosen by NCSA as the master licensee of NCSA Mosaic. They will license Enhanced NCSA Mosaic to other vendors, who will then distribute copies to end users. Spyglass is committed to maintaining a single code base for all three Mosaic platforms and keeping a consistent interface across all platforms. Thus, all three versions should be consistent in their reliability and functionality, which has not been true in the versions on the Net.

Enhanced NCSA Mosaic for Windows features a number of improvements over the original NCSA version, including:

- Dramatically faster performance

- Reduced memory requirements—one-half to one-third the memory previously required

- Easier installation

- Support for printing

- Simplified interface for easier browsing

- Support for forms, allowing for two-way communication between users and Web servers

- Proxy gateway support for security in networked environments

- Online help system.

NCSA is now focusing on research into advanced features for the next generation of Mosaic, such as voice recognition, full-motion video, and intelligent agents for searching on the Internet. NCSA will continue to offer a public-with-copyright version of Mosaic over the Internet, which you can download for free. As part of the NCSA-Spyglass agreement, Spyglass will provide many of its improvements to NCSA, which will incorporate them into their version.

Support and Registration

This book includes version 1.0 of Enhanced NCSA Mosaic. New versions are expected to be available, and we can provide them online to registered users. Be sure to complete the online registration form accessible from the Mosaic Handbook Home Page. Check the Mosaic Handbook Support Center to learn about updates to the program.

If you have problems with the software, check the online Support Center. If you cannot solve your problem using the online resources, you can send email to *support@gnn.com*. We generally cannot deal with the specifics of your Internet connection beyond what we describe in Chapter 2. Be sure to ask your system administrator or your Internet service provider if you are having problems using Mosaic to access documents on the Internet.

The Home Page

The disks that come with this book also include the Mosaic Handbook Home Page, which is the first document you see when you start this version of Mosaic.

During the installation process, the Mosaic Handbook Home Page will be copied to your computer's hard disk. The Home Page contains links to the *Global Network Navigator*, the *Mosaic Handbook Hotlist*, which provides online links to all the Internet resources mentioned in this book, and the Mosaic Handbook Support Center. It also has a link to a document that allows you to register your copy of Enhanced NCSA Mosaic. These resources are *not* on the disks shipped with this book; they are on the Internet. If you don't have an Internet connection up and running, you will not be able to access these resources.

The Home Page provides an easy way for you to start using the World Wide Web and the Internet. Later in the book, we will show you how to modify the Home Page and add links to your favorite resources.

Throughout the book, we'll refer to the Mosaic Handbook Home Page as your Home Page (with initial capital letters) to distinguish it from other home pages in general. Most servers have a home page, which is the first document you come to when connecting to a server. We'll refer to these pages by their full names, such as the NCSA Home Page.

The Mosaic Handbook Hotlist

Because filenames and server locations change with great frequency, we have created the *Mosaic Handbook Hotlist*. This document will be maintained on the *GNN* server (rather than included on the disks) so that it can be updated if the network addresses of the resources described in this book change. Online access will also make it more convenient for you because you don't have to type the long addresses yourself.

Conventions

The following font conventions are used in this book:

Italic	is used for file and directory names, USENET news-groups, and to emphasize new terms.
Bold	is used for commands, command-line options, hypertext links, and Internet names and addresses.
Constant Width	is used for HTML tags and the contents of files or the output of commands in examples.
Constant Italic	is used within examples for variables that the reader will replace with an actual value.
Constant Bold	is used within examples for text that is literally typed by the user.

Acknowledgments

This book was produced as the result of a collaborative effort over a fairly short period of time. Ron Petrusha provided an early draft of the book, and a number of other people contributed throughout the process. In particular, we'd like to thank the entire staff of *GNN*, who are responsible for developing the Internet's premier Web site. We'd especially like to recognize Joan Callahan, Ellie Cutler, John Labovitz, Jennifer Niederst, and D.C. Denison. Joan, Ellie, and John contributed to Chapter 3. In Chapter 8, we used articles that D.C. wrote for *GNN* to describe the World Wide Web organization. Jennifer, *GNN*'s Art Director, designed the Mosaic Handbook Home Page and its supporting documents.

Richard Koman did a terrific job of coming in under pressure to help get this book together. He wrote chapters 2, 4, 5, 6, and 7. Dale Dougherty, publisher of *GNN*, wrote chapters 1, 3, and 8. Paula Ferguson did a great job of reviewing the book and adapting it for the X Window System, rewriting chapters 5 and 6 and revising chapters 2 and 4.

Clairemarie Fisher O'Leary steered the book through production, and caught a few errors of ours based on her own knowledge of HTML. Stephen Spainhour shared the production duties in getting the various versions of the book into print. Edie Freedman designed the cover art, capturing our navigation theme. Chris Reilley handled the illustrations throughout the book. Frank Willison, O'Reilly's Managing Editor, coordinated this effort and kept us on track. Chris Tong and Susan Reisler did the indexing. Frank Howard captured the screenshots for the Windows version. Valerie Quercia wrote the glossary. Lenny Muellner and Jessica Hekman provided technical support. Sheryl Avruch and Sue Willing also provided invaluable help with various production and administrative tasks.

Thanks also to Tim O'Reilly, whose company has made it possible to grow in so many interesting and worthwhile directions.

CHAPTER ONE

THE WIDE WORLD OF INTERNET SERVICES

What Is the Internet?
The Internet and Online Services
The Client and the Server
The Development of WWW and Mosaic
Developing the Global Network Navigator

Without the Internet, Mosaic wouldn't make much sense. Using Mosaic on a computer that's not connected to the Internet is like having a car that sits in the driveway. Before you go to visit the many services that the Internet has to offer, there are a few things you should know about this global network.

This chapter contains basic information about the Internet, which is useful for understanding how Mosaic works. It explains the client/server architecture behind most Internet information services. We also examine the development of the World Wide Web and how Mosaic came to be. If you find yourself itching to get started, please feel free to jump ahead to the next chapter. This chapter isn't "required reading" because it contains information that most people on the Internet already know.

What Is the Internet?

Not so long ago, if you asked "What is the Internet?" you'd get a technical answer. A longtime Internet user would usually make the following points:

- The Internet is a network of networks, with millions of computers connected to one another.

- The TCP/IP protocols at the core of the Internet describe how messages are addressed and sent as packets from one computer on the network to another. A packet may be routed through several computers to reach its destination.

- The Internet came into being as a U.S. Defense Department network, ARPAnet, that was designed to withstand a nuclear bomb attack. It is a distributed network without a vulnerable central hub.

- The National Science Foundation (NSF) built a network, NSFNET, on the same model as ARPAnet to connect research and educational institutions. Because of the government funding, commercial traffic was restricted by an Acceptable Use Policy. In the early 1990's private, commercial networks joined the Internet, and restrictions on commercial activity were relaxed.

Today, the Internet has come to mean something much more than a physical network with historical ties to research, education, and national defense. It has become a cultural icon, emblazoned on the cover of *Time* magazine, and the subject of many stories in your hometown newspaper and *The Wall Street Journal.* The Internet has come to represent what the future looks like today, and to suggest what is possible when people can communicate with each other around the world.

The Internet has been variously characterized as the Information Superhighway, the Infobahn, and Cyberspace. It has been called the best reason to have a personal computer at home. John Markoff of *The New York Times* has written that the PC, not the set-top box, will rule the consumer market and that services such as those provided on the Internet will be available sooner and prove more valuable than video-on-demand and 500-channel cable systems.

So, what do people do on the Internet? They exchange email, follow newsgroups, and download files. They also find information and other people. These are things that many people have done for years on traditional online services such as CompuServe and America Online. What's so fascinating about the Internet? How does it differ from these online services?

The Internet Is Distributed

You could say that CompuServe is a big computer and hard disk in Columbus, Ohio. CompuServe users dial in via modems to access that computer and its data. It is a centralized network, completely owned and operated by CompuServe.

The Internet, in contrast, is completely distributed. Your computer connects to another computer that is connected to another computer. The TCP/IP protocol ties it all together invisibly, so you don't need to know exactly how your data gets from one computer to another halfway around the world. You are accessing not one computer, but many. You connect to your Internet service provider and from that point you can access any computer on the network.

The Internet Is International

Perhaps the most exciting thing about the Internet is its sheer size. While the Internet has its origins in America and most Internet traffic originates here, it is a global network. The fact that we can retrieve a document from Switzerland, Germany, Japan, or New Zealand demonstrates that we live in an interconnected global community.

The Internet Is Wide Open

Nobody really runs the Internet—at least not yet. Some have compared the Internet to the Wild West, with arguments escalating into flame wars instead of gunfights. There are few rules, at least written ones, but there is a culture that tends to support and enforce its wishes.

The Internet is wide open in a technical sense. Nobody owns the Internet, and there is little proprietary technology involved in its operation. This means that people have lots of choices.

The Internet and Online Services

One of the most interesting developments on the Internet is its potential to redefine how we obtain online services via a public network. The Internet effectively unbundles the services that a traditional online service provides; that is, the charge for network access is separated from the charge for content. For instance, a customer of Mead Data, which provides Lexis and Nexis online services, uses a private network, a software interface, and a delivery system, all built and maintained by Mead Data in order to supply the content to their users. Users pay high hourly rates for the amount of time they are on Lexis or Nexis accessing content.

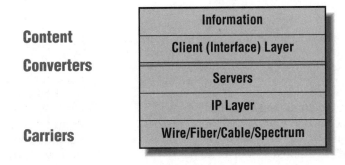

Figure 1-1. Layers of the Internet

Figure 1-1 shows the layers of the Internet. Each layer may be supplied by a different vendor. At the bottom is the carrier, the wire over which the bits are transmitted. These are typically phone lines leased from the local and national phone companies, but the carrier can also be a cable company.

The next layer up from the bottom is the *IP* (*Internet Protocol*) layer. Each Internet service provider has a network of computers that it serves, and it routes Internet traffic to and from those machines. At the next layer, you have client and server software. In short, the server software distributes information on the Net, while users run client software to access and display that information.

A traditional online service often supplies a single interface program—usable only with that service. On the Internet, you have lots of tools to choose from, including programs to exchange email, participate in newsgroups, and search and gather information. In many cases, there are shareware or public domain versions of these programs as well as more fully featured, commercially supported programs. The point is that there are many sources that can supply you with an Internet connection and the kinds of tools that you use while connected.

Because the Internet is a general-purpose network that has many uses, a company might install an Internet connection just as it does a phone system. It allows users within the company to communicate with the rest of the world. The general-purpose network serves those who want access to information as well as those who want to provide information to others. In fact, with this information infrastructure in place, it becomes easier and cheaper to become an information provider, so more people can do it. That has great potential for revolutionizing the business of online information services.

The Client and the Server

A key to making Internet information services more accessible is making them easier to use. For many users, their first experience with the Internet was a UNIX command-line prompt:

```
unix%
```

At this prompt, the user would type in various commands such as "who am i" or "ftp" or "rlogin."

Until recently, UNIX was the interface of the Internet and you had to learn something about the UNIX command set to navigate successfully. UNIX is a very powerful operating system (and the Internet, as well as O'Reilly & Associates, owes a lot to UNIX), and networking is part of its basic design. From the very beginning UNIX computers were networked to each other, and programmers found useful ways to take advantage of the benefits. On UNIX systems, many programs were designed with a client/server architecture, which means that a program was divided into two parts that could run on different computers.

Take a word processing program as an example. Imagine that all the file handling routines are executed on a computer dedicated to that task. This software is the *server*. On your personal computer, meanwhile, a program controls the user interface and responds to your interactions. This is the *client*. When you ask for a file, the client program sends a message to the server to send that file. The server complies with the request, and the client then interprets and displays the file.

In other words, the server software on one computer manages the information and access to it, and the client program on another computer manages the user's interactions with the information.

One exciting aspect of client/server design is that multiple clients can interact with a single server or with many different servers. In addition, clients can fit into the user's environment and assume the likeness of other locally run programs.

In short, this means that Windows users can run a Windows client that interacts with servers on powerful UNIX machines. As a user, you get the benefit of using a client that fits into your computing environment, while accessing a central file server that can handle lots of requests at once.

Mosaic is client software, and there are Mosaic clients for the Windows, Macintosh, and X Window System environments. All three programs receive the same information from the server, but they may display it differently. Mosaic is specifically designed to access World Wide Web servers, but it can also access other types of information servers.

Information Servers

An Internet-based information server is a computer that runs a program to handle incoming requests for information. There are actually many different types of information servers on the Internet. In this section, we will survey FTP, Gopher, and WAIS. Each provides a different way to access information, and user interactions range from the simple to the arcane. When we get to the World Wide Web in the next section, you will better understand how information access can be even easier.

FTP

If you run an *FTP* (*File Transfer Protocol*) server, you allow users on other computers to log on to your computer and retrieve files that you have put in a public area. Since giving each user an account would be a problem, an FTP server is set up to accept anonymous logins.

When O'Reilly & Associates first published our computer books, we made sample source code available on our FTP server. One server that we use for this is **ftp.ora.com**. We told our readers how to come in using the Internet to retrieve the files. Below you can see a sample FTP session, in which, after logging in, we change directory (**cd**) and then use the **get** command to retrieve the file named *bookcat.txt*.

```
dale % ftp ftp.ora.com
Connected to ruby.ora.com.
220 ruby FTP server (Version wu-2.4(1) Fri Apr 15 14:14:30 EDT 1994) ready.
Name (ftp.ora.com:dale): anonymous
331 Guest login ok, send your complete e-mail address as password.
Password:
230-Welcome to O'Reilly & Associates, Inc. FTP Archive.
230-
230-If your ftp client chokes on this message, log in with a '-' as the
230-first character of your password to disable it.
```

```
230-
230-If you have problems with or questions about this service, send mail to
230-ftp-manager@ora.com; we'll try to fix the problem or answer the
230-question.
230-
230-Current local time is Mon Aug 1 00:02:24 1994
230-
230 Guest login ok, access restrictions apply.
ftp> cd /pub
250-This directory includes...
250-
250-book_covers Image files of the covers of O'Reilly's books
250-book* Book catalog in four different formats
250-errata/ Errata and updates for various O'Reilly titles
250-examples/ Example files and programs from O'Reilly publications
250-
250-"Index" files in this directory and subdirectories have more information.
250-
250-Please read the file Index
250- it was last modified on Thu Jul 21 08:44:06 1994 - 11 days ago
250 CWD command
successful.
ftp> get bookcat.txt
200 PORT command successful.
150 Opening ASCII mode data connection for bookcat.txt (124651 bytes).
226 Transfer complete.
local: bookcat.txt remote: bookcat.txt
127533 bytes received in 31 seconds (4 Kbytes/s)
ftp> quit
```

The advantage of FTP is that any kind of file can be made available, whether ASCII text, PostScript, or various graphics formats. Almost anyone on the Internet can access a file via FTP, although the commands make it feel like a lot of hard work. If you know what you want and where it is located, then FTP works reasonably well.

Gopher

Gopher originated at the University of Minnesota, where the varsity is known as the Golden Gophers. Gopher made things easy for users looking for information, as well as for organizations wanting to provide information. From the user's point of view, information on a Gopher server is organized as a series of hierarchical menus. Using a Gopher client, you choose a particular item on a menu and receive either a submenu or a text file.

Putting up a Gopher server requires not much more effort than running an FTP server. You arrange files in a set of directories, with each directory corresponding to a menu of choices presented to the user. At O'Reilly & Associates, we set up a Gopher server to provide information about our books. You can access this

Gopher server by running the Gopher client on your local machine. The UNIX command for this is:

```
unix% gopher gopher.ora.com
```

There are different Gopher clients available, including several commercial clients for Windows and the Macintosh. Here is the opening screen from our server:

```
Internet Gopher Information Client v2.0.12

Root gopher server: gopher.ora.com

--> 1. About O'Reilly & Associates
    2. News Flash! -- New Products & Projects/
    3. Detailed Product Descriptions/
    4. Ordering Info/
    5. Complete Listing of Titles
    6. FTP Archive & Email Information/
    7. Feature Articles/
    8. Errata for "Learning Perl"/
    9. Bibliographies/

Press ? for Help, q to Quit Page: 1/1
```

Gopher was responsible for the first big surge in Internet traffic as people began exploring what was available on servers throughout the world. Anyone can quickly understand how to move through the network of Gopher servers.

Unfortunately, what Gopher gained in ease of use, it lost in flexibility. Users felt as though they were always moving from one menu list to another, and when you finally got somewhere, you ended up with a ASCII document that wasn't very enjoyable to read.

WAIS

WAIS (*Wide Area Information Servers*) was developed by a consortium of four companies interested in designing an easy-to-use searching system. The consortium, consisting of Thinking Machines Corp., Apple Computer, Dow Jones, and KPMG Peat Marwick, was lead by Brewster Kahle, then at Thinking Machines in Cambridge, Massachusetts. Brewster saw that there was so much information available on the Internet that anyone would have trouble locating the most relevant documents.

Each WAIS server contains a full-text index of all the documents on the server. A user of a WAIS client submits a simple query, such as a keyword or phrase, and the WAIS server returns a list of the documents that contain those words. If you select one of the documents from the list, it will be displayed on your computer.

Although WAIS was originally developed for use with a graphical client on the Apple Macintosh, in practice most people do not use a WAIS client. They access a WAIS server using either a Gopher client or a WWW client. Therefore, searching for a document has become an alternative to browsing. For instance, on the O'Reilly Gopher server, you can access a WAIS server to perform a keyword search of the book descriptions online. This is what a WAIS query looks like:

```
+----------------------Keyword search on Descriptions----------------------+
| |
| Words to search for |
| _____ |
| |
| |
| [Help: ^_] [Cancel: ^G] |
+---------------------------------------------------------------------------+
```

If we enter the keyword "Internet" in the search field, WAIS will return a list of books whose descriptions contain that word. The result looks like this:

```
Keyword search on Descriptions: Internet

--> 1. !%@:: A Directory of Electronic Mail Addressing & Networks
    2. Computer Security Basics
    3. Connecting to the Internet: An O'Reilly Buyer's Guide
    4. DNS and BIND
    5. European Networking
    6. Global Network Operations
    7. Learning the UNIX Operating System
    8. Mobile IP Networking
    9. Networked Information and Online Libraries
    10. Notable Speeches of the Information Age, John Perry Barlow: USENIX
Conferen..
    11. Security and Networks
    12. TCP/IP Network Administration
    13. The Future of the Internet Protocol
    14. The Whole Internet User's Guide & Catalog
    15. Volume 6A: Motif Programming Manual
```

Selecting any book by number will display the book's description. Note that WAIS tries to rank the list in order of importance, but you usually have to scan the list and select the most appropriate choice. For instance, the book that is most clearly about the Internet, *The Whole Internet User's Guide and Catalog*, shows up 14th on the list.

WAIS is a valuable tool for indexing large bodies of information and helping users locate specific documents in a collection. However, most users do not find searching alone to be an intuitive way to work. Therefore, WAIS servers typically run alongside other servers.

For more information about information servers and how to set them up, see *Managing Internet Information Services*, by Cricket Liu, Jerry Peek, Bryan Buus, Russ Jones, and Adrian Nye, published by O'Reilly & Associates.

The Development of WWW and Mosaic

The World Wide Web is very similar in design to the Internet-based information servers we examined in the last section. However, WWW offers several advances, including a document-oriented view of computing that offers formatted text and graphics instead of menu lists.

The World Wide Web at CERN

The World Wide Web originated at the European Particle Physics Laboratory (CERN) in Geneva, Switzerland. Tim Berners-Lee, an Oxford University graduate who came to CERN with a background in text processing and real-time communications, wanted to create a new kind of information system in which researchers could collaborate and exchange information during the course of a project. For most scientists, a publication presents a record of what a project accomplished; that is, you read it after the project is long over. Tim saw the need for physicists to collaborate in real time, and not just on one project, but on many.

Tim used hypertext technology to link together a web of documents that could be traversed in any manner to seek out information. The web does not imply a hierarchical tree, the structure of most books, or a simple ordered list. In essence, it allows many possible relations between any individual document and others. Tim implemented hypertext as a navigational system, allowing users to move freely from one document to another on the Net, regardless of where the documents are located.

The term "hypertext" was coined in the 1960's by Ted Nelson, who defined it as "non-sequential writing." He wanted to emphasize that hypertext applied not only to locating and reading information, but also to creating it. Nelson popularized the idea in his books and his vision of a global hypertext system called Xanadu. This was a project designed to remain incomplete, rather like building a library to contain all the world's information. Surprisingly, the World Wide Web comes as close to realizing Xanadu as anything Nelson and his associates have achieved, though Nelson has argued that WWW lacks several key aspects of his system.

While the WWW does present a navigational model that is much easier for users, it also presents some problems for information providers. It requires authoring documents in a particular format defined by the system. Specifying a document format is necessary if hypertext links are to be embedded in the document.

There were many implementations of hypertext systems before the World Wide Web. What Tim did, in cooperation with others at CERN, such as Robert Caillau, was to define an Internet-based architecture using open, public specifications and free, sample implementations for both clients and servers. Because the specifications are public, anyone can build a client or a server. Because there are sample implementations and the code can be obtained for free, developers can choose to build or refine parts of the system. Both factors encourage other people to contribute to the project, and as is true of many things on the Internet, the WWW effort has turned into a collaborative project involving people and organizations from around the world.

WWW specifications

Let's look briefly at the WWW specifications. While this is not necessary for you to become a Mosaic user, it will help you understand how Mosaic works.

The World Wide Web is a set of public specifications and a library of code for building clients and servers. There are three key specifications:

- URL (*Uniform Resource Locator*)

- HTTP (*HyperText Transfer Protocol*)

- HTML (*HyperText Markup Language*)

Figure 1-2 illustrates how these specifications work together. A URL is the address of a document on a network server. If a user clicks on a link in a document that contains a URL, the client interprets the URL and then initiates a session with the specified server. HTTP is the protocol, a fixed set of messages and replies, that both the client and server understand. Thus, the client sends a message to the server requesting a document and the server returns it. The document itself is coded in HTML, and the browser interprets the HTML to identify the elements of the document and to render it. The use of HTML allows documents to be formatted for presentation using fonts and line justification appropriate for the system on which it is displayed.

The format of a URL is discussed in Chapter 2, *Getting Started with Mosaic*. The HTTP protocol is not discussed further in this book. The basics of HTML are covered in Chapter 7, *Creating HTML Documents*.

Early Browser Development

The team at CERN implemented a line-mode browser, which is the lowest common denominator among browsers, and can be used from almost any kind of terminal.

```
Welcome to the World-Wide Web
THE WORLD-WIDE WEB

This is just one of many access points to the web, the universe of
information available over networks. To follow references, just type the
number then hit the return (enter) key.

The features you have by connecting to this telnet server are very primitive
compared to the features you have when you run a W3 "client" program on your
own computer. If you possibly can, please pick up a client for your platform
to reduce the load on this service and experience the web in its full
splendor.
```

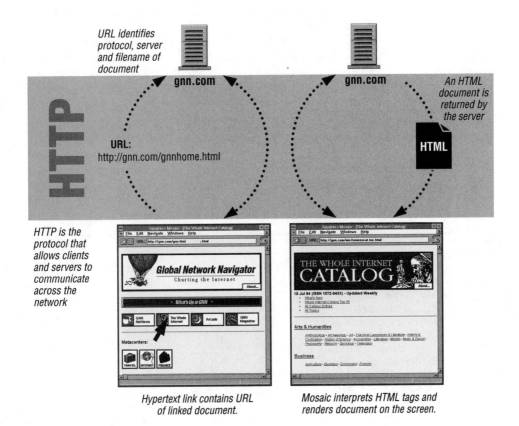

URL identifies protocol, server and filename of document

gnn.com

URL:
http://gnn.com/gnnhome.html

gnn.com

An HTML document is returned by the server

HTML

HTTP is the protocol that allows clients and servers to communicate across the network

Hypertext link contains URL of linked document.

Mosaic interprets HTML tags and renders document on the screen.

Figure 1-2. How Mosaic retrieves a document

```
For more information, select by number:

A list of available W3 client programs[1]
Everything about the W3 project[2]
Places to start exploring[3]
The First International WWW Conference[4]

This telnet service is provided by the WWW team at the European Particle
Physics Laboratory known as CERN[5]
[End]
1-5, Up, Quit, or Help: q
```

The example above shows the initial login session with the line-mode browser, using TELNET to access the CERN server (**info.cern.ch**). As you can see, the screen is formatted ASCII text. Links are numbered and appear inside brackets. To follow a link, you enter the number of the link at the prompt at the bottom of the screen.

Another browser with a better interface was developed for Steven Jobs' NeXT computer. However, it did not receive wide usage outside CERN. Lynx, a browser with a full-screen interface, was developed at the University of Kansas by Lou Montulli. This is what a sample screen from the *Global Network Navigator* (*GNN*) using Lynx looks like:

```
GNN Directory

Global Network Navigator

[1][News]  [2][Whole Internet Catalog]  [3][Arcade]  [4][Magazine]
_____

Metacenters:

[5][Travel Center]  [6][Internet Center]  [7][Finance Center]
_____

Market Resource Centers:

[8]USENIX Association
[9]Lonely Planet Publications
[10]Mountain Travel*Sobek
[11]The Company Corporation
[12]Digital Equipment Corporation
[13]Heller, Ehrman, White, & McAuliffe
[14]Mobile Fidelity Sound Lab
[15]O'Reilly & Associates, Inc.
[16]Bolt Beranek and Newman


[17]Advertiser Index


_____

[18][What's Up in GNN]  [19][Subscribe]

All original text and graphics copyright (c) 1994 O'Reilly & Associates, Inc.
```

In some ways, when the first versions of Mosaic became available in the spring of 1993, WWW had reached proof-of-concept stage but it had not achieved widespread use. While multiple clients existed, none of them suggested the potential of combining text and graphics in a graphical Web client. With an easy-to-use interface that lets you click on a link to navigate the Web, as well as the ability to display graphics, Mosaic made the Internet accessible to a broader group of users.

The Development of Mosaic at NCSA

The National Center for Supercomputing Applications (NCSA), located at the University of Illinois at Urbana-Champaign (UIUC), was funded by the National Science Foundation to provide supercomputing resources to the research community.

NCSA was part of a wider effort by Congress to fund a national infrastructure for high-performance computing and communications.

It would be nice to write that such government funding directly resulted in the development of Mosaic. However, Mosaic came about rather unexpectedly. Marc Andreessen was an undergraduate student at UIUC, who had a part-time job at NCSA, building tools for scientific visualization. He began working on Mosaic as one of those tools, but pretty soon he knew he was onto something bigger. From that point on, Marc was racking up far more hours than his part-time status required. Eventually, Eric Bina joined Marc in developing Mosaic.

To Marc's credit, when he started building Mosaic, he looked around on the Internet and discovered that he didn't have to start from scratch. He found the WWW and saw that it was intended to serve a community similar to the one served by NCSA. Having an existing code base available from CERN meant his work could progress very quickly, even if he had to re-write some of the code to make it usable.

It is hard to point out any single new feature that Mosaic introduced, either as a hypertext browser or a WWW client. Rather, Marc made available a solid program with the right number of features for users to feel amazed and empowered by their ability to navigate the riches of the Internet. Figure 1-3 shows Mosaic viewing the same *GNN* page that was shown before with Lynx.

Marc was not only the developer of Mosaic, he was also its champion. He spent lots of time on the Web developer mailing list, talking about various development issues. He introduced minor improvements, and sometimes major changes, overnight, and sent out new versions for immediate distribution on the Net. While many people anxiously awaited the updates, NCSA wasn't sure what Marc had created, and where it fit inside their organization. Nonetheless, the excitement of government supporters, the press, and the Internet user community was overwhelming. NCSA expanded its Mosaic development efforts, hiring students to develop Windows and Mac versions.

With the April 1993 release of Mosaic 1.0 for the X Window System, Mosaic began to drive the explosive growth of the World Wide Web. By that fall, Version 2.0 of Mosaic for X came out, and the first beta versions of WinMosaic and Mac Mosaic were released.

Commercialization and Future Developments

NCSA is not a commercial software development organization; it was chartered to create software for scientific researchers and place it in the public domain. NCSA made Mosaic freely available on the Internet "for academic, research, and internal business purposes only." No doubt these terms have helped make Mosaic popular. Anyone can get a copy, try it out, and realize how useful it is. Naturally, commercial software developers have taken notice of Mosaic. Many of them are interested in taking its development further.

Figure 1–3. Sample Mosaic screen

Because Mosaic is copyrighted, anyone wanting to modify the source code or distribute binaries of Mosaic must obtain a license to do so from NCSA. Initially, NCSA handled the licensing of Mosaic. In August 1994, NCSA announced that it had reached an agreement with Spyglass, Inc., to have them serve as the licensing agent for Mosaic.

As a result of the various licensing deals by companies that will continue development of Mosaic, we may wind up with many different versions of Mosaic. *The Mosaic Handbook for Microsoft Windows* comes with Enhanced NCSA Mosaic, developed by Spyglass, which we chose because it is likely to define the core feature set for Mosaic.

In the long run, NCSA Mosaic may be viewed as the application that made the Internet important, just as Lotus 1-2-3 created a market for IBM personal computers. Others are at work on products that will compete with Mosaic, including Marc Andreessen himself. Marc left NCSA in December 1993 and eventually founded a company with James Clark, one of the founders of Silicon Graphics, Inc. Mosaic Communications Corp. has hired many of the original Mosaic developers from NCSA, and it will be interesting to see what they create in light of such high expectations.

Developing the Global Network Navigator

At O'Reilly & Associates, we had been looking at various methods of publishing online. After all, we wrote books about computers, and it seemed to make sense to deliver books about computers on computers. We had developed a number of requirements for online publishing and as we began learning about the World Wide Web, we got very excited. At the time, we were just about to publish Ed Krol's *The Whole Internet User's Guide and Catalog*, which would become a bestseller.

We began to explore the Web and wonder what uses a publisher could make of it. One of our first efforts was an online demo of the resource catalog in the Krol book. It was so well received that we began to think of making it into a product, and that led to the development of the *Global Network Navigator*. Using a Web server to put the resource catalog online was the obvious part of it; we also saw the opportunity to create online magazines. The magazine format could be used to portray what people were doing on the Internet, what they were interested in.

As Mosaic became available in the summer of 1993, we began doing demos and showing people just what was possible with the new technology. In fact, we had to take great pains to make people understand where Mosaic ended and *GNN* began—that Mosaic was intended to retrieve documents from network servers and that we ran a network server ready to deliver our documents upon request to Mosaic users.

We launched *GNN* in August 1993 at the Interop tradeshow in San Francisco, and it officially went online October 1. We made *GNN* available for free, but asked that users register and become subscribers. As of September 1, 1994, we have over 50,000 subscribers.

GNN introduced advertising in our online publications. We make it possible for advertisers to deliver a message in an editorial context that we have created for users. We also think, perhaps ambitiously, that we can change the nature of advertising by asking advertisers to take advantage of this new medium and provide users with only as much information as they are interested in receiving. We call it "content-driven" advertising.

That is all said to give you some flavor of *GNN* as a pioneering effort in online publishing, an ongoing experiment in creating online audiences. As it grows, *GNN* will continue to change, making it difficult to describe on paper, especially using black-and-white screenshots. The real thing is online and in living color. Online, *GNN* may differ some from what you see in this book, but it is a good way to show off the capabilities of Mosaic and to help you explore the World Wide Web.

GETTING STARTED WITH MOSAIC

Now that you understand something about how Mosaic, the World Wide Web, and the Internet all fit together, we can start using Mosaic to explore the Web. This chapter will show you how to navigate the Web using hypertext, Mosaic's controls, and Internet path names (called URLs). Once you understand the basic navigation techniques, you can traverse the Web to visit an incredibly wide variety of information sources all over the world.

We assume that you are familiar with the Windows environment, so we don't cover the basics that can be found in any Windows manual. Before getting started, however, we must make sure you are on the Internet and have the right kind of connection to use Mosaic. You can't get started without it.

The Right Kind of Internet Connection

Perhaps the most difficult part of using Mosaic for the new user is understanding how to obtain the right kind of Internet connection. Fortunately, it is getting a lot easier to get an Internet connection these days, especially if you know which applications you want to use, such as email and Mosaic.

In this section, we give an overview of your options for getting on the Internet. If you want more detail, consult Susan Estrada's *Connecting to the Internet: A Buyer's Guide*, also from O'Reilly & Associates.

First of all, you need to find a local *Internet Service Provider* (*ISP*). The ISP essentially maintains a computer network of customers who are connected to the Internet through their computer. There are two major lists of Internet service providers—the Public Dialup Internet Access List, or PDIAL, maintained by Peter Kaminski, and Susan Estrada's Internet Access Provider List, or DLIST. To get a copy of PDIAL, send an email message to **info-deli-server@netcom.com** with the text "Send PDIAL" in the body of the message. For information about getting the DLIST, send email to **dlist@ora.com**.

Before you contact an ISP, you should decide which type of connection is best for you. You need to make an assessment of your needs and what you can afford. (It is similar to buying a computer in that regard.)

There are basically three kinds of Internet connections: dialup shell, PPP/SLIP, and dedicated lines.

Dialup Shell Account

> A dialup shell account is usually the cheapest and easiest type of connection you can get. Unfortunately, you can't use Mosaic over that connection. (You have to run a browser such as Lynx on your Internet host computer.)

PPP/SLIP Account

> A PPP/SLIP account usually runs over a high-speed modem (14,400 or 28,000 bits per second, or bps) that connects to your ISP. The main difference between a shell account and a PPP/SLIP account is that the latter puts your computer on the network. Both operate over standard phone lines, and both require you to dial up and connect to an ISP. However, to use a shell account, you typically use a telecommunications program to dial the Internet host and log in. If you have PPP or SLIP, these programs establish the connection and you can then route Internet traffic to and from your machine.

> PPP/SLIP also provides an important piece of the connection puzzle—TCP/IP, the protocols that allows data to traverse multiple networks on the way to its final destination. With a PPP/SLIP account or a dedicated line connection you will be able to use Mosaic just fine.

> While PPP/SLIP connections over fast modems offer reasonable speed, they are still quite a bit slower than dedicated lines, so it's best to get as fast a modem as possible. While you can use a 9600 bps modem with Mosaic, it will seem rather slow. Anything less than 9600 baud is unacceptable.

Dedicated Line

> Many organizations connect to the Internet via a dedicated line, which is a separate telecommunications line that connects you to your ISP. Both of you have a piece of equipment known as a router that routes the traffic between your local area network and the computer network maintained by your ISP. Dedicated lines come in various speeds; the slowest is a 56K line, which is four times faster than a 14.4K bps modem.

Peak Performance

When you use Mosaic to retrieve a document from the Internet, there are a number of factors that affect performance. You may click on a link and not get an immediate result. If you understand that your computer is responsible for only a portion of the final result, then you may be more patient. Here are some of the factors affecting performance:

- The speed of your Internet connection

- The amount of traffic on the Internet, which includes all points between you and your destination

- The load on the server from which you are retrieving the document, perhaps along with thousands of other users at the same time

- The size of the document, which often depends on whether or not you are retrieving documents with graphics, or even larger data objects, such as sound or video files

Of these factors, only the first one is really within your control. You may be able to get a higher speed connection by obtaining a faster modem, using ISDN if available, or making arrangements for a dedicated phone line into your business.

Installing Mosaic

If you have your connection worked out, you're ready to install Mosaic. One of the advantages of Enhanced NCSA Mosaic is that installation is quite simple. Here's how to do it:

- Insert Disk 1 in your floppy drive and type:

    ```
    a:setup
    ```

- The Mosaic Setup Program will launch and automatically install Win32s on your computer. Win32s allows you to run 32-bit programs such as Mosaic on your PC.

- You will then be asked to insert Disk 2. The setup program will ask you to verify the path for Mosaic. It should look something like this:

    ```
    C:\WIN32APP\EMOSAIC\EMOSAIC.EXE
    ```

- Click **OK** to approve the path.

The program will then install Mosaic. When installation is complete, you will see a new program group and program item for Enhanced NCSA Mosaic.

Starting Mosaic

Now you're ready to use Mosaic to start navigating the Web. Launch Mosaic by double-clicking on its icon in the Program Manager. Mosaic starts by opening a home page, or start-up document. Your version of Mosaic comes with a special home page created just for this book. You copied this document, the Mosaic Handbook Home Page, from the floppy disk to your hard disk when you installed Mosaic. If you are not connected to the Internet, Mosaic will still display the Home Page, but not before displaying a message saying that the network did not initialize properly. If you are using a modem, make sure that PPP or SLIP is able to connect to your Internet Service Provider. PPP and SLIP can be difficult to configure correctly, so talk to your ISP if you're having a problem.

If your organization has an Internet connection and multiple local area networks (LANs) but you can't reach the Internet, you may be on a LAN that isn't configured for TCP/IP. If this is the case, you may need to gateway from your LAN to the TCP/IP LAN, so you can access the Internet. Talk to your network administrator about how to accomplish this.

If things are working correctly, you won't see the network error message. You will see the home page banner, some introductory text, and several graphics that provide links to Registration, *GNN*, the *Mosaic Handbook Hotlist*, and Mosaic Support. We'll begin our introduction to Mosaic by clicking on these links and exploring some of the resources on *GNN*.

The Mosaic Interface

Before we get started, let's take a minute to get familiar with the Mosaic interface. Some of these will be discussed in more depth later in the chapter, so at this point we'll move quickly through the interface.

It is important to make a distinction between Mosaic itself and the document it is displaying. In Figure 2-1, Mosaic is displaying the Home Page in the document window, but the Home Page is not part of Mosaic. Mosaic displays the title of the active document in the title bar. In this example, the title is "Mosaic Handbook Home Page."

Beneath the menu bar is the toolbar. The two arrows at the left let you navigate back and forth among recently viewed documents. The field labeled "URL" displays the Internet address of the current document. The S-shaped icon at the right activates when Mosaic is busy retrieving a file.

At the bottom of the screen is the status message area, which displays messages about what Mosaic is doing. To the right is a progress indicator bar, which shows (roughly) Mosaic's progress in downloading documents.

The uses of these elements will become clear as we start using the program.

Figure 2–1. Mosaic Handbook Home Page

Connecting to GNN

To get started with Mosaic, let's visit *GNN*. You'll notice that the GNN icon on the Home Page is surrounded by a heavy border, as are the other icons. That tells you that it's a hypertext link. Click on it to go to *GNN*. Mosaic then goes out on the

Internet and downloads the *GNN Home* page. When it's finished, it displays the formatted page—complete with graphics—on your screen, as shown in Figure 2-2.

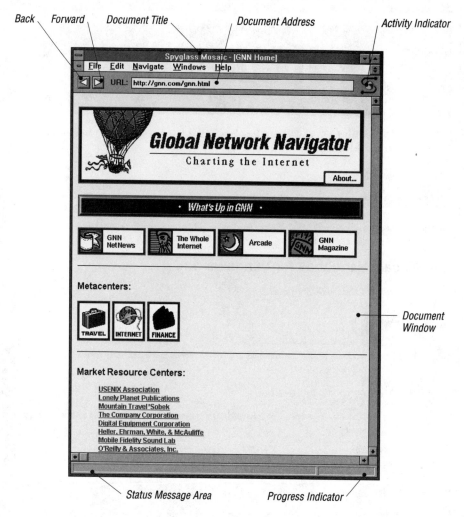

Figure 2–2. Elements of Mosaic's interface

Each of the graphics on the *GNN Home* page is surrounded by a border, so you know that they're hypertext links. Try clicking on the **What's Up in GNN** bar near the top of the page. After a little while, the *What's Up in GNN* page will display.

A Look at GNN

Congratulations, you've just mastered the most important navigation skill for using Mosaic and the World Wide Web. Clicking on hypertext links is also the easiest and most enjoyable way to navigate the Web. By just clicking on links, you can explore the Web by following subjects and ideas that interest you, discovering new areas of interest in the process. Hypertext links one document to another, which is linked to another, and so on, through literally thousands of documents. This system of links gives the World Wide Web its name; the links are like threads in a spider's web, connecting all the different servers together into a single system. Some servers, like the NCSA and CERN servers, have huge numbers of links pointing to them; others have relatively few. Now that you have hypertext down, let's throw in one of Mosaic's navigation tools. From the *What's Up* page, click on the **Back** arrow (the one pointing to the left) to go back to the *GNN Home* page. Clicking on the **Back** arrow tells Mosaic to display the last document you were looking at.

Let's take a more in-depth look at the *GNN Home* page. Under the *GNN* banner are icons for various centers in *GNN—What's Up in GNN, The Whole Internet Catalog, GNN Business Pages, NetNews*—as well as *GNN*'s special publications, the *Travelers' Center*, the *Personal Finance Center*, and the *Digital Drive-In*. You can visit any of these centers by clicking on the graphic.

At the bottom of the page is a graphic labeled **Subscribe to GNN**. You can click here to fill out a subscription form, which helps us learn who is using *GNN* and what parts of the service are most useful. Let's get started by going to *NetNews*, shown in Figure 2-3. Click on the **NetNews** graphic, and Mosaic gets and displays the *NetNews* home page.

Multimedia in Mosaic

The *GNN* pages integrate text and graphics in one document. These graphics are called *inline graphics* because they are displayed in the document. You can also view full-size images and photographs, animations and video, and listen to sound files. Mosaic cannot display these files directly but relies on "viewer" programs to display them.

Often you'll see a postage stamp-size graphic that is also a link. This image may be linked to a full-size version of the image, which can be displayed in a graphics viewer program. Other links may take you to video, audio, PostScript files, and many other kinds of files. We'll discuss multimedia in more depth in Chapter 6, *Using Mosaic for Multimedia.*

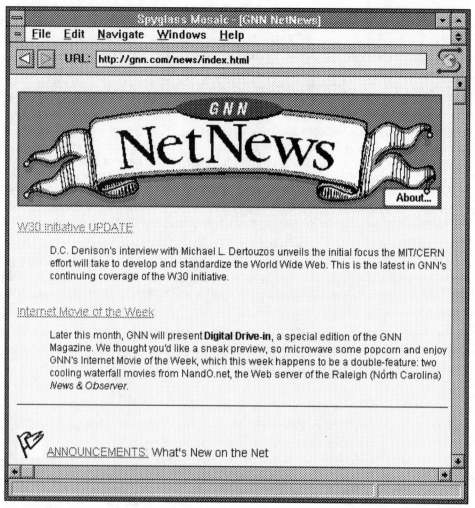

Figure 2-3. GNN NetNews

Getting Your Page

How does hypertext work? Basically, when you click on hypertext—whether it's text or graphics—you are telling Mosaic that you want to see the document that is linked to the hypertext. When you clicked on the **NetNews** graphic, you told Mosaic that you wanted to see the *NetNews* page.

But how does Mosaic know, of all the millions of documents on the Internet, which page is the *NetNews* home page, where it is, or how to get it? It knows because every hypertext link has embedded in it a URL that gives the name of the computer where the document is stored, the path and name of the document, and the protocol for transferring the document. Every computer on the Internet has a unique name and every document has a unique URL.

When you click on the **NetNews** graphic, for instance, a number of things happen:

- Mosaic looks up the URL for that link, in this case, *http://gnn.com/news /index.html.*

- Mosaic opens an HTTP (the Web protocol) connection to the *GNN* server.

- Mosaic sends the URL to the server to request the *NetNews* home page.

- The *GNN* server sends the *NetNews* home page, which is an HTML (HyperText Markup Language) document. HTML is a simple tagging language that tells Mosaic how to format the document on your computer.

- Often, as with this page, the HTML document includes instructions for graphics files to be displayed at certain positions on the page. Mosaic contacts the server again to download the graphics files.

- When all the related files have been received, Mosaic interprets the HTML tags and displays the document on your computer.

If this all seems complicated, you can be grateful that Mosaic shields you from so much of it. As a Mosaic user, you don't need to know which document you're asking for, what computer it lives on, where that computer is, what the protocol is, or any of the many other things Internet users used to have to know. All you need to be able to do is click on a hypertext link and wait for the document to be delivered.

Mosaic's Navigation Tools

As you link your way around the Web, you'll make the online equivalent of a wrong turn and you'll want to go back where you came from. Other times, you'll find some pages you really like and want to return to often. And you'll probably forget many of the places you've been, but you may want to revisit some of them.

Mosaic provides tools to deal with each of those situations, to give you more control over your Mosaic session than you could possibly have just by following links. The major tools are:

- **Back** and **Forward** buttons (found on the **Toolbar**)

- **History** (found in the **Navigate** menu)

- **Hotlist** (found in the **Navigate** menu)

Using **Back** and **Forward** is like walking around your neighborhood—it's the quickest way to get to your neighbor's house. **History** is like driving your car on the interstate—you have to start it up and pay attention to the exit signs, but it's the best way to cover distance. Finally, the **Hotlist** is like taking a plane to your destination—you have to make arrangements first but once you do, you'll get where you're going in a flash.

Back and Forward

To check out these tools, let's return to *NetNews*. At the top of the page are two news story headlines. (*NetNews* is a constantly changing section, so the version you see when you connect will be different than the version printed here.) Click on the top headline, **W3O Initiative Update**, to read that story. The article, which is reprinted in Chapter 8, *Future Directions*, is shown in Figure 2-4. After you read this article, you may want to go back to the *NetNews* page. To do so, click on the **Back** arrow in the top left corner of the toolbar. Now click on the second headline and Mosaic will display the "Internet Movie of the Week" article. Again, clicking on the **Back** button takes you to back to *NetNews*. But if you click on the **Back** button again, you'll return to the W3O article. That's because you're moving back in the order that you viewed different documents. You were looking at the pages in this order:

1. NetNews

2. W3O article

3. NetNews

4. Internet Movie of the Week

So, starting from "Internet Movie of the Week," clicking **Back** takes you to *NetNews*, then to the W3O article, then back to *NetNews* again, and then back to *GNN Home*.

The **Forward** button works in the same way. From *GNN Home*, clicking the **Forward** button takes you to *NetNews*, "W3O," *NetNews*, and "Internet Movie of the Week."

Hotlist

A hotlist is Mosaic's way of letting you save a list of your favorite Web sites. Once you've added a page to your hotlist you can go right to it by selecting the entry in your hotlist. Let's take a look at how this works.

Using the **Back** and **Forward** buttons, return to the W3O article. This is a fairly long article, so you might want to return to read it later. To make it easily accessible, you can add the article to your hotlist. Under the **Navigate** menu, you'll see the option **Add Current Document to Hotlist**. Choosing this option adds the article to your hotlist.

Figure 2–4. *W3O Initiative Update*

Now let's take a look at the hotlist. As you can see in Figure 2-5, the only document in the hotlist is the one we just added. When you select that document, the URL appears at the bottom of the **Hotlist** dialog box. As you add more documents to your hotlist, they will appear in the list window. To go to a document on your hotlist, select the title and click on **Go To**.

The **Hotlist** dialog also has several options for managing your hotlist. **Add Current** does the same thing as **Add Current Document to Hotlist**. **Delete** removes documents from the list.

Hotlist also has something unusual—a powerful command called **Scan Current**. When you click on this button, Mosaic takes all the URLs from your current

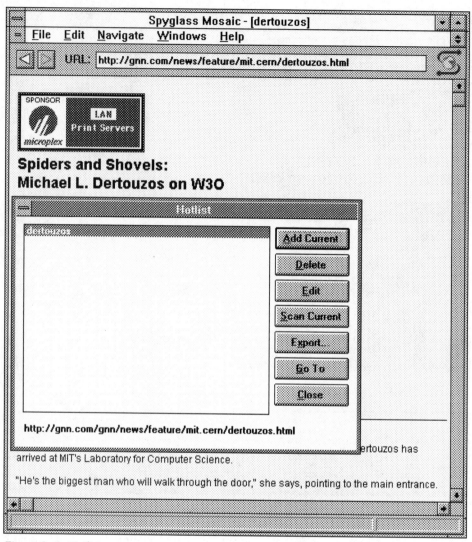

Figure 2–5. Hotlist

document, finds their titles, and adds them to your hotlist. Then you can go right to any of those documents by double-clicking (or using the **Go To** button) on their titles. Since we're looking at the W3O article, clicking on **Scan Current** takes all the links within that page and adds them to the hotlist. Figure 2-6 shows what the hotlist looks like after doing this. This has two advantages. First of all, after you've moved on to another page, you won't have to go back to the original and click on the hypertext to get to the document; just go to **Hotlist** and choose it from the list. Secondly, you'll be able to see the title and URL of the document in the **Hotlist** window, which may give you more information than the hypertext does.

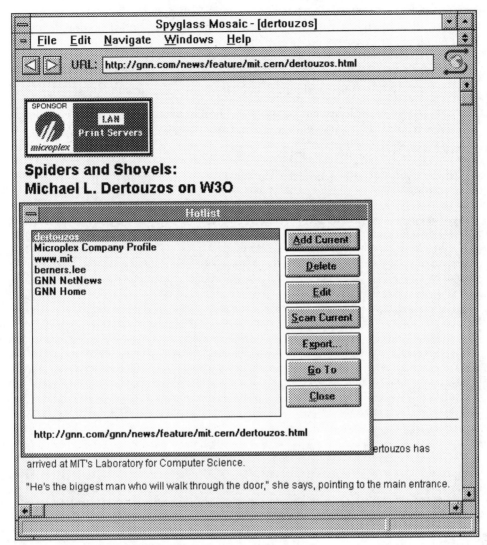

Figure 2–6. Hotlist with Scan Current list

You can also edit the selected entry, using the **Edit** command. With **W3O** selected, click on the **Edit** button. Another dialog box will appear with fields for the **Title** and for the **URL**. If you want, you can change the title of the document here.

You could also edit the URL here. The only reason you would want to is if a document's URL changes. Usually the server will maintain a document at the old URL, which points to the new document. In this case, add the new document to your hotlist and delete the old one.

Next is the **Export** button. This lets you create a Web document on your computer that contains hypertext links to all the documents in your hotlist. **Export** lets you keep multiple hotlists. For instance, try this:

1. With **W3O** as your active document, choose **Hotlist** from the **Navigate** menu.

2. Choose **Scan Current** to add all the links from that page to the hotlist.

3. Now go back to **Hotlist** and export the hotlist to a document on your hard disk. Give the file a name with an *.htm.* extension, such as *W3O.htm.*

4. Your new hotlist page will display, as shown in Figure 2-7.

5. Choose **Add Current to Hotlist.** You can now open your hotlist page from the **Hotlist** dialog.

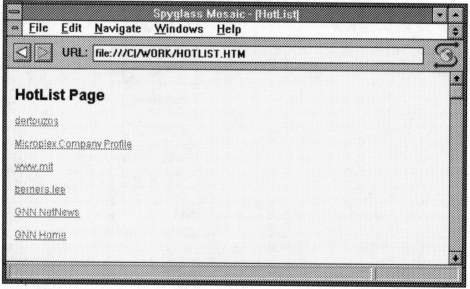

Figure 2–7. Hotlist exported to document

History

By the time you've read some of the articles in *NetNews* and visited some of *GNN*'s metacenters, you've been to quite a few places. You probably didn't add to your hotlist all of the documents you might want to look at again. But you don't have to retrace your steps from scratch in order to find those documents. You can use the **History** feature to revisit places you've been.

If you want to go back to the W3O article, for instance, just choose the **History** option from the **Navigate** menu. Select **W3O** and click on **Go To.** Mosaic displays that document. The **History** dialog box, shown in Figure 2-8, contains all the documents you've ever visited, not just the ones you visited in the current session. That makes it quite a powerful tool because you don't have to worry about how to get back to a document you saw a week ago.

On the other hand, it won't take long before your history list is quite unwieldy. To trim it down, use the **Delete** button to remove unwanted documents. All the other buttons in **History** are identical to the ones in **Hotlist**.

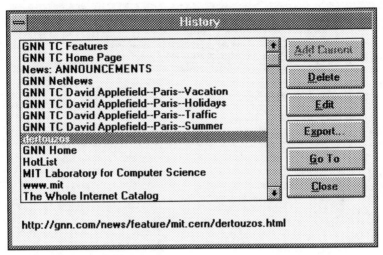

Figure 2–8. The History dialog box

Entering URLs

When you know the URL of a document you want to see, you can enter it directly. For instance, to get to *GNN Home*, you can enter the URL *http://gnn.com /GNNhome.html*, as shown in Figure 2-9. This has the same effect as clicking on a link to that document or choosing it from a hotlist or history window. All navigation techniques do essentially the same thing—use a URL to identify a document.

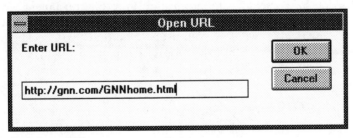

Figure 2-9. Entering a URL

You don't necessarily have to have the full URL to use **Open URL**, however. If you know the directory, you can usually get an index of it by ending the URL with a slash. For instance, try entering this URL: *http://gnn.com/meta/travel/features/*. Figure 2-10 shows the results, an index of all the files in the *Travelers' Center* features directory.

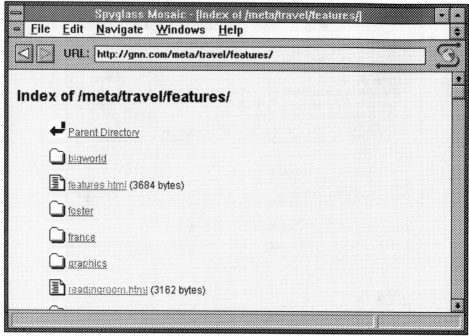

Figure 2–10. Listing of the Travelers' Center's features directory

Finding Text

If you're looking for some specific information in a long document, you can use Mosaic's **Find** command to search for a text string. Choose **Find** from the **Edit** menu, which brings up a window with a text field and two checkboxes, one to match case and one to search from the top of the page. To search, enter the text string in the field and click **OK**.

Saving and Printing

Mosaic not only lets you navigate around the Net to view documents, it also lets you print documents and save them on your own computer. Both are simple operations.

If you want to print a Web document, just select **Print** from the **File** menu. Mosaic will print the page, with graphics in place. Regardless of the dimensions of the application window, Mosaic will print your page so that if fits neatly on letter-size paper. Mosaic is set to print with .75" margins on all sides, so it will print the page at a width of seven inches. For information about changing the margins, see Chapter 5, *Customizing Mosaic.* If you're switching between printers or need to make other changes in your printing setup, use the **Page Setup** and **Printer Setup** options under the **File** menu.

You can save a text version of the document by using the **Save As** option from the File menu, as shown in Figure 2-11. For instance, if you really like one of the "Big World" articles from the Travelers' Center, you can save it to your hard disk so you can read it offline. If you want plain text, set the File Type pop-up menu to **Text Files**, which saves the file with a *.txt* extension. If you want to save the HTML coding, choose **HTML Documents**, which saves the file with a *.htm* extension.

You can also preview and save HTML documents by using the **View Source** option from the **Edit** menu. For more information about HTML, see Chapter 7, *Creating HTML Documents.*

There is no easy way of saving inline graphics on your PC. If you are intent on doing so, you can write down the URL of the graphic as Mosaic downloaded it, then enter that URL using the **Open URL** command. You can then save the file to your disk. Another option would be to take a screenshot of your Mosaic window and cut and paste the graphics into separate documents.

The fact that you can download text and graphics brings up the subject of copyright. Remember that, even though this information is on the Net, it is someone's intellectual property and may be protected by copyright laws. If you're building your own Web documents and want to include someone else's work, it's a simple matter to include a hypertext link to the work, as described in Chapter 7.

In general, you should feel free to save or print a Web document for your own personal use. Copyright issues tend to arise when you distribute a copy of the document or make additional copies.

NOTE

If at any point you want to stop a transmission, just press the **ESCAPE** key. You will see an error message saying that Mosaic cannot connect to the server. Click **OK** and continue.

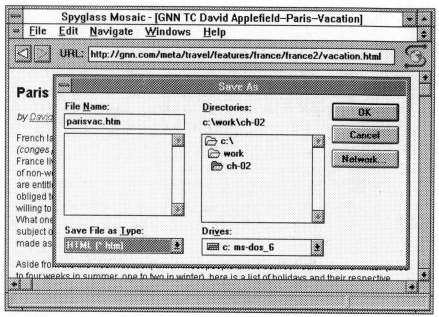

Figure 2–11. The Save As dialog box

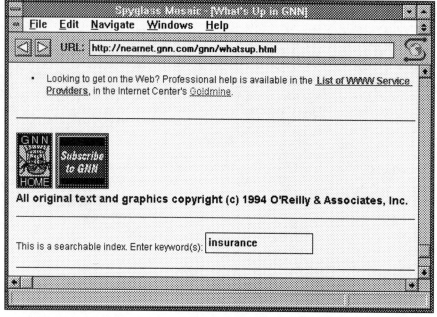

Figure 2–12. Searching the contents of GNN

Document-Based Features

Many Web servers offer features beyond simply viewing text and graphics. Two common features are the ability to search a database and to fill out and send a form back to the server.

Searching

As we discussed earlier, you can search an individual document using Mosaic's **Find** command. But some servers offer a much more sophisticated searching function that lets you search the full text of all documents on the server. These servers use the Wide Area Information Servers (WAIS) system to provide this searching capability.

GNN offers the ability to search all the documents in *GNN* using this system. On certain pages of *GNN*, you will see the message, "This is a searchable index. Enter keyword(s):" followed by a blank field. To search *GNN*, you type the words you are looking for in the field and press **Return**, as shown in Figure 2-12.

Let's say you're searching for articles about insurance. Type "insurance" into the field and in a few seconds you'll receive a list of documents that have something to do with insurance. Each item in this "hitlist," shown in Figure 2-13, is a hypertext link that you can click on to retrieve the document. The server considers this

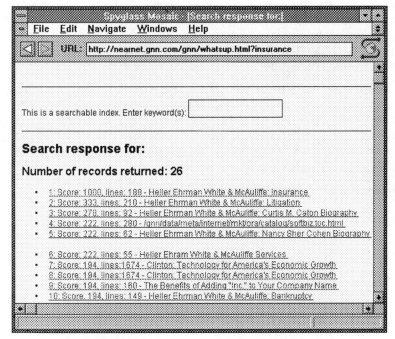

Figure 2-13. Search results are returned as a list of hypertext items

list to be in descending order of relevance. Depending on the results you get, you may beg to differ. One important concept to remember about this kind of searching is that you are searching the full text of every document—not just descriptions of documents. Also remember that you are searching all of *GNN*, not just the center you are in at the time, and only the contents of *GNN*. For information about servers that search the Web, see Chapter 3, *Exploring the World Wide Web*.

Filling Out Forms

Some Web documents are actually forms that you can fill out and return to the server. The *GNN Registration Form* is one of these. As you go through it, you'll notice that sometimes there are blank fields for you to fill out and sometimes you're asked to pick one of several items. Filling out forms is a fairly intuitive process, as you can see from Figure 2-14. Using your mouse to move from one field to another, fill in the appropriate text. Before you go on to Chapter 3, take the time to register your copy of Mosaic and become a subscriber to *GNN*. To get to the registration page, go to your Home Page and click on the **Register** link.

Understanding URLs

As we discussed earlier, Mosaic uses URLs to get the documents you ask for, whether you click on a link, enter a URL, or use Mosaic's tools like **Hotlist** and **History**. URLs are the *lingua franca* of the Web. When you find a great new server, you can tell your friends about it by passing along the URL. In fact, there are several mailing lists devoted to announcements about new services. When we talk about Web servers and documents, we talk about their URLs. Although you can get to the servers mentioned in this book by clicking on the links in the *Mosaic Handbook Hotlist*, we also provide the URLs so you can enter them directly.

A URL consists of three main parts: the protocol, the hostname (which is not required in all URLs, although it is for HTTP), and the document's pathname. To use a driving metaphor, the protocol tells Mosaic what kind of road to take, the hostname tells it what exits to take, and the pathname gives directions for getting to a specific location The URL for the *GNN Travelers' Center* is *http://gnn.com/meta /travel/index.html*. This follows the syntax for URLs:

```
protocol://server/directory/filename
```

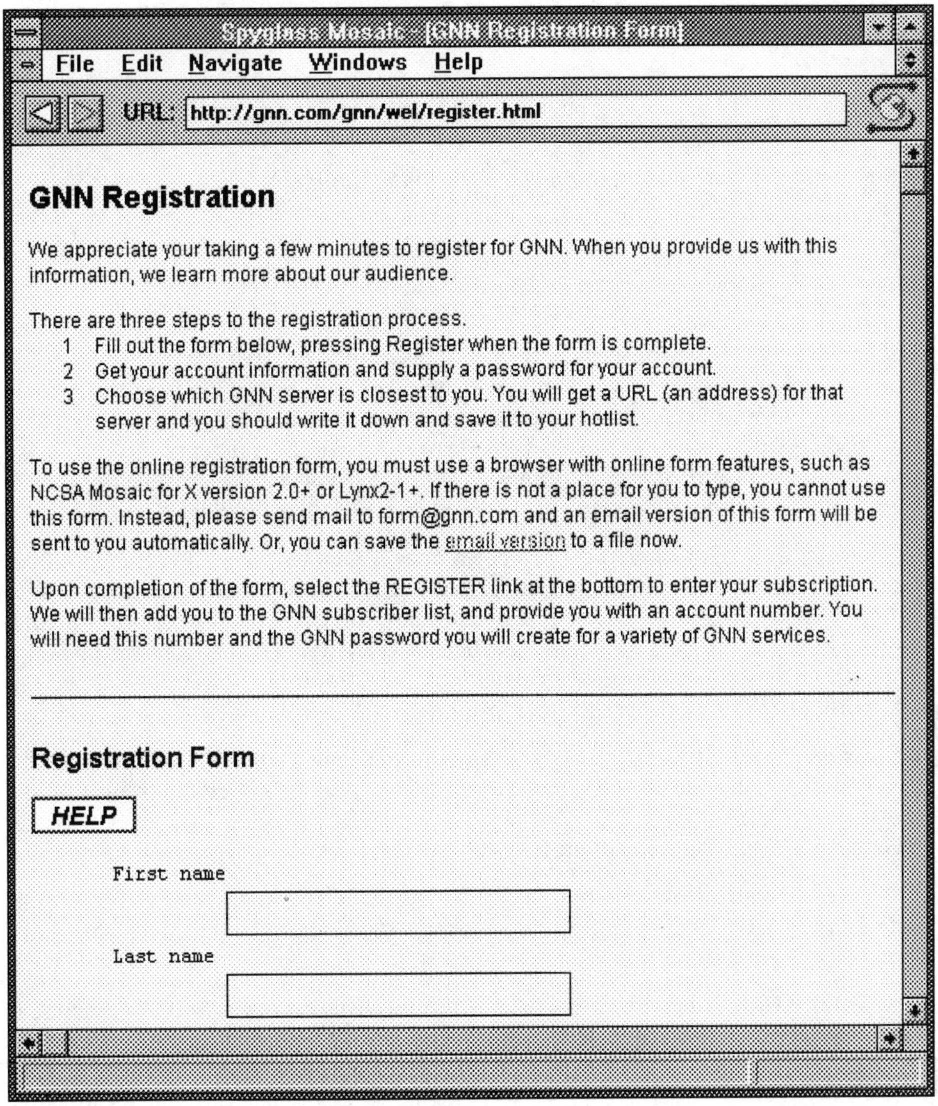

Spyglass Mosaic - [GNN Registration Form]

File   Edit   Navigate   Windows   Help

URL: http://gnn.com/gnn/wel/register.html

GNN Registration

We appreciate your taking a few minutes to register for GNN. When you provide us with this information, we learn more about our audience.

There are three steps to the registration process.
1   Fill out the form below, pressing Register when the form is complete.
2   Get your account information and supply a password for your account.
3   Choose which GNN server is closest to you. You will get a URL (an address) for that server and you should write it down and save it to your hotlist.

To use the online registration form, you must use a browser with online form features, such as NCSA Mosaic for X version 2.0+ or Lynx2-1+. If there is not a place for you to type, you cannot use this form. Instead, please send mail to form@gnn.com and an email version of this form will be sent to you automatically. Or, you can save the email version to a file now.

Upon completion of the form, select the REGISTER link at the bottom to enter your subscription. We will then add you to the GNN subscriber list, and provide you with an account number. You will need this number and the GNN password you will create for a variety of GNN services.

Registration Form

HELP

First name

Last name

Figure 2–14. GNN Registration Form

Table 2-1 shows the parts of the URL and the corresponding parts of the *Travelers' Center* home page.

Table 2-1: Anatomy of a URL

URL	*http://gnn.com/meta/travel/index.html*
Protocol	*http:*
Host Indicator	*//*
Server	*gnn.com*
Pathname	*/meta/travel/index.html*

You'll notice that this URL starts with *http*. This is the protocol for the World Wide Web. Whenever you contact a Web server, the URL will start with *http*. But Mosaic also works with other Internet applications, so sometimes you'll see a URL that starts with *gopher*, *wais*, or *ftp*. In those cases, Mosaic is contacting one of those non-Web services and presenting the results to you in Web format. (See Chapter 4, *Accessing Other Internet Services*, for more about these information services.)

A colon appears right after the protocol name. It signals the end of the protocol name. Next come two slashes, which indicate that a hostname will follow. (When sharing Web URLs in conversation, it's customary to spell out this part of the URL: "h-t-t-p-colon-slash-slash," unwieldy as that is. *GNN* writer D.C. Denison has suggested that this URL prefix should be abbreviated to "hittip" in conversation, but that shorthand doesn't appear to have caught on.)

The next part of the URL is the server name, in this case *gnn.com*. On the Internet, most computers end in *.com* for commercial sites, *.edu* for educational institutions, *.gov* for government agencies, or *.net* for network providers. By checking the server's extension, you can get an idea of what kind of server you're contacting.

The server name is followed by a directory path, which uses slashes (not backslashes, as in DOS and Windows) to separate directories; in this case, the pathname is */meta/travel*.

Note that the URL ends with *.html*. This is the file extension for Web documents. It stands for HyperText Markup Language, a tagging scheme that lets authors create hypertext documents. When you see this file extension, you know you're receiving a Web page and not a directory or some other kind of file. Documents in other applications may have other file extensions. As you probably know, DOS and Windows only allow three-character file extensions, so Web documents created on these systems will have an extension of *.htm*.

When Things Go Wrong

Sometimes when you try to open a connection, things don't go quite right. For instance, it might take a *really* long time to connect to the server. It may be that you're connecting to a distant server and it's just going to take a long time. Or you may be dealing with a slow or overburdened network. If the server is actually down, you'll eventually get an error message from Mosaic that the connection failed.

People often change the locations or names of their documents, which means, of course, that the URL has also changed. The more polite folks out there will leave a document that points to the new URL. If not, however, you'll simply get an error message that the URL couldn't be found.

You'll also get an error message if you make a mistake when entering a URL in the **Open URL** field. If this happens, check the URL and try again. Remember you can use Windows' copy-and-paste functions to avoid typing out URLs. Then, if it still doesn't work, you can go back to the person who gave it to you and give him or her what for.

The thing to remember about Mosaic and the Web is that when things don't work out, it's hardly ever your fault. Just accept the fact that you can't get access right now and try again later.

Now you know the basics of using Mosaic to navigate the Web. In the upcoming chapters, we'll talk more about customizing Mosaic, using other Internet services with Mosaic, and taking advantages of Mosaic's multimedia capabilities.

CHAPTER THREE

EXPLORING THE WORLD WIDE WEB

The Ages-old Problem of Navigation
The Global Network Navigator
Mosaic Handbook Hotlist
Other Lists and Resource Guides
Searching the Web

Coming to the Internet for a new user is like arriving in a new country without a map or a guidebook. Mosaic makes it easy to get almost anywhere you want to go on the Net. However, the more difficult part is knowing what places are worth visiting and where they are located. This is especially true on the World Wide Web. Each information server has its own interface or navigational system. Some are highly structured, and others are very loosely organized. That there is such variety as you move from one server to another is one of the fascinating aspects of the Web. But navigation can be confusing and you can get lost.

To explore the Web, you have to know where to look, and the *Global Network Navigator* is a good place to start. *GNN* provides several useful navigational guides for Mosaic users, such as *The Whole Internet Catalog*. There's also the NCSA Mosaic *What's New* page. We will start by using these guides to discover public resources that are available.

In Chapter 2, *Getting Started with Mosaic*, we used *GNN* to demonstrate how the Mosaic interface works. In this chapter, we are going to demonstrate how to use *GNN* itself. We have also organized a tour of the Internet, using selections from *GNN's Best of the Net* award-winning sites to introduce different forms of servers. We will show examples of servers organized as online exhibits, magazines, and kiosks.

As you get more experience using Mosaic to explore the Internet, you will no doubt find your own ways to locate information sources, and you will discover how you best like to navigate from one server to another. As you get out on your own, you'll want to investigate the numerous search facilities described in this chapter that index information on the Web.

The Ages-old Problem of Navigation

On the Internet, information is everywhere. Knowing where to look to find the right information is a challenge. There are thousands and thousands of servers worldwide, with hundreds being added every month. How do you find the servers that have the information you are most interested in? How do you learn more about them and where they are located? How do you know when a new server comes online that might interest you? These are the basic problems of Internet navigation.

Navigation is an ages-old challenge that people must face as they enter unfamiliar territory by land or water. The problem is one that can be solved if you have good information, and, throughout the ages, navigational guides for all kinds of people and every form of travel have been published. One of the first books published in the American West, when Pittsburgh was on the frontier, was called *The Navigator*, by Zadok Cramer. The first edition was published in 1802, and it described how to make the journey from Pittsburgh down the Ohio River. It pointed out significant features used to measure distances between places, explained how to avoid numerous hazards, and described what to look for when buying a boat.

The Navigator was written for immigrants and traders, people new to the frontier who had never made the journey down the Ohio River. *The Navigator* brought together the experiences of those who made their living on the river, and organized them in a compact form for use by newcomers.

Just as *The Navigator* helped settlers navigate the American frontier, *GNN* is helping people find their way across the terrain of the Internet. The writers and editors of *GNN* have spent a lot of time on the Internet, probably more time than you want to spend yourself. We know where to look and we try to keep up with the dynamic growth of information services on the Internet. *GNN* organizes access to the Internet by creating a variety of publications that will help you pursue your interests and spend your time more productively.

If you'd like to know more about significant trends and the interesting people on the Net, read *GNN NetNews*, which contains new feature stories and commentary each week. In Chapter 8, *Future Directions*, you can read a story from *GNN Net-News* that explains the new WWW organization, W3O, and has an interview with one of its organizers.

GNN's special interest areas, called metacenters, have publications aimed at specific audiences, those who enjoy travel or want to learn more about personal finance, for example. In the *GNN Travelers' Center*, you will find articles by real-world explorers who send in their dispatches to us.

The Internet is a new communications medium, which is one reason for all the excitement about it. What is so exciting to us, as creators of *GNN*, is that the information you need to navigate the Internet successfully can be effectively presented to you via the Internet.

The Global Network Navigator

Let's get started (finally!) by going to *GNN*. As shown in Chapter 2, you can access *GNN* by any of the following methods:

- From the **GNN** menu, select **GNN Home**.

- From the Home Page, click on the link to *GNN*.

- From the **File** menu, choose **Open URL** and type in the URL for *GNN*.

  ```
  http://gnn.com/GNNhome.html
  ```

You are retrieving the *GNN Home* page from one of *GNN*'s information servers on the Internet. (Just to be clear, this page is not on the disk shipped with this book, nor is it on your own hard disk. It is out on the network, and if you can't reach the network, you will get an error message.) The time that it takes to retrieve this page will vary depending on the speed of your connection and other factors.

When Mosaic retrieves the *GNN Home* page, you will have a document that serves as a directory to *GNN*'s publications and special-interest areas. When you choose any of the links on this page, you will download another document from the *GNN* information server. If you choose a publication, you will go to its front page.

NOTE

The figures that we use in this book may differ from what you actually see online in *GNN*. This is because *GNN* is dynamic, and there is always new information. We also restructure *GNN* periodically to accommodate new ideas or services.

One of the links on the *GNN Home* page is to the *What's Up in GNN* page. If you click on this link, you can find an itemized summary of new things that are happening in *GNN*. An example of that page is shown in Figure 3-0. On the *What's Up* page, each item describes a feature to be found somewhere in *GNN*. You can select any of the links and go directly to a publication, for instance, or to a document in any of the publications. For now, just scroll to the bottom of the page. On the bottom, you will see a colorful icon labeled "GNN HOME," as shown in Figure 3-1. This is a navigational icon that will take you back to the *GNN Home* page, where we started. Click on it now to return to our directory of publications. (Of course, you could also use the **Back** button to return to the previous document.)

Navigational icons are but one example of how an information server can provide a system of navigation for its users. For instance, if you get lost in *GNN*, look for the navigational icons at the bottom of a page. They can take you to major sections of *GNN* or back to the home page. Similarly, if you don't see any of *GNN*'s navigational icons, then it is probable that you have retrieved a document from another server. In *GNN*, we have explicitly labeled links that take you out of *GNN*

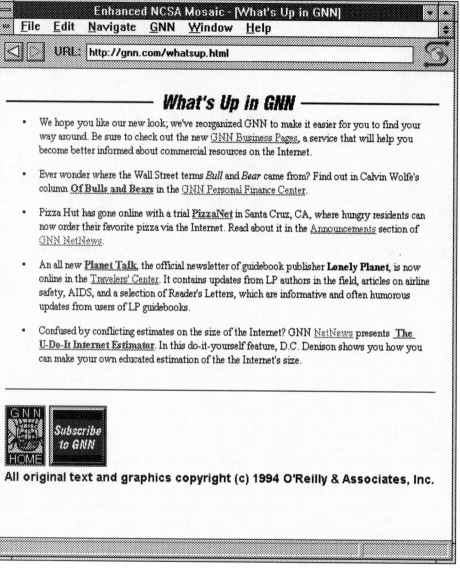

Figure 3-1. The What's Up in GNN page

Figure 3-2. GNN Home navigational icon

to other servers. These are called "GO" links, and there is a **GO** button or label that you click on to traverse the link. When you link to a server outside of *GNN*, you go to another information space, and you have to figure out what the rules of navigation are for that server. You can always get back to *GNN* by using the **Back** button. You will see more examples of navigational choices as we explore *The Whole Internet Catalog*.

Before beginning the next section, click on the link for **The Whole Internet** on the *GNN Home* page and open this publication.

The Whole Internet Catalog

The Whole Internet Catalog is organized by subject. It is selective rather than exhaustive in its listings of resources. We don't list absolutely every resource on the Net; instead we list the ones that we believe are the best. Our editors check out resources and evaluate them for inclusion in the *Catalog*. (We provide some pointers later in this chapter to listings that attempt to be exhaustive.)

The Whole Internet Catalog began as a sampler of Internet resources that appeared first in print in *The Whole Internet User's Guide and Catalog* by Ed Krol, published by O'Reilly & Associates. We put this catalog online and expanded it, keeping it more up-to-date than any print listing could be. Each entry in the *Catalog* describes an Internet resource, and provides a link to the resource that allows you to go there directly.

Let's look at a few examples. The front page of the *Catalog*, as shown in Figure 3-3, has a distinctive masthead followed by several links, which we'll discuss later, that gives you alternative views of the catalog. The main view is a listing of subject categories. You may need to scroll down the list to see all the subject categories. You can navigate from the main subject listings or more detailed, second-level subject categories. If you are interested in Art, click on that link. You will go to a list of information servers that specialize in Art. Here is a sample list:

```
Art

    Ansel Adams Photographs
    Architecture, etc.
    Art History in Australia
    ASCII Clipart Collection
```

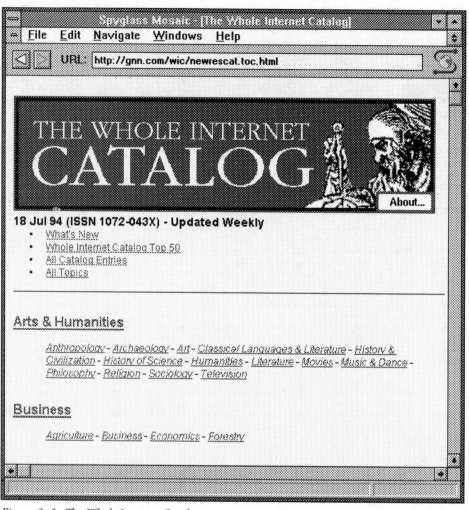

Figure 3-3. The Whole Internet Catalog

```
Black Artists at the National Museum of American Art
Bodleian Library MSS
The California Museum of Photography
Computer Images & Art
Japanese Art
Kaleidospace
Strange Interactions
Krannert Art Museum
The Ohio State University at Newark, Art Gallery
OTIS
A Roman Palace in ex-Yugoslavia
Smithsonian Institution
Vatican Library MSS Exhibit
```

Each name in this list is a link to a catalog entry that describes the server and what it offers. These entries are like cards in a library's card catalog system, describing an online information service. Now, we will select three different servers from the *Catalog* and visit them.

The Palace of Diocletian at Split

Each entry contains a description of the server, as well as links that take you to it. If you choose "A Roman Palace in ex-Yugoslavia," then you go to the entry for that server, as shown in Figure 3-4. The entry for the Palace at Split shows two links because the information is found on two different servers. Choose the

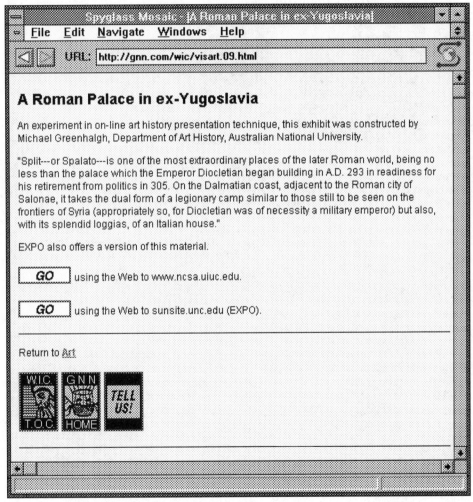

Figure 3–4. The Whole Internet Catalog entry for the Palace of Diocletian at Split

second **GO** link (the first one is to a more experimental version) and you'll go to this server to retrieve the document shown in Figure 3-5.

Figure 3–5. The home page for the Palace exhibition

Let's make sure you understand what happened. You used *The Whole Internet Catalog* to choose an information service and traverse a link that takes you directly to that server. The document in Figure 3-5 is not part of *GNN*; it is a separate resource. This document contains lots of links to additional information, but it does not contain a link back to *GNN*.

The Palace of Diocletian at Split is an online interactive exhibit. After you have read the introductory text on this page, follow the link at the bottom of the page to the palace. The document, shown in Figure 3-6, is the main navigational document for this exhibit. An image at the top of the page contains buttons that you can click on to visit different areas of the exhibition. You may notice a difference

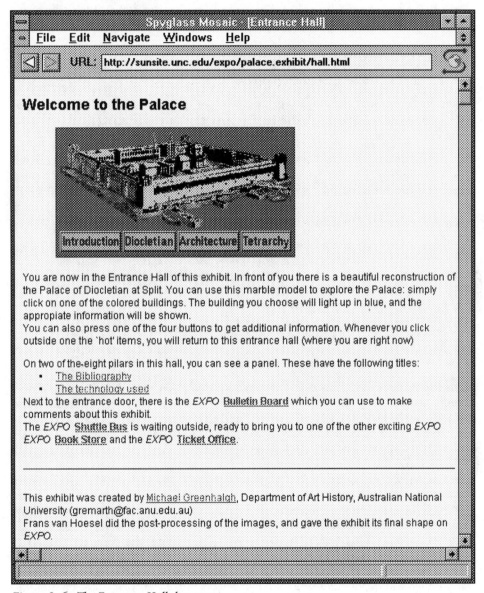

Figure 3-6. The Entrance Hall document

between the buttons found on the graphic and other buttons that you find on a page. These buttons are mapped as specific hot regions on the graphic, and when you click on one of them, the Mosaic browser sends a message to the server giving the coordinates of the region in which you clicked. It then returns a document whose URL has been mapped to that region. (Because of the HTML tag associated with this process, a navigational graphic is known as an ISMAP graphic.) You may also notice that when you move from one button to the next on this graphic, the destination URL that is displayed in the Status box does not change.

If you click on the button labeled **Introduction**, you can begin the exhibit. At the end of the page for each document in the exhibit, you will find the same graphic and you can use it to explore other topics.

When you are done, use the **Back** button to get back to *GNN*. Of course, if you have gone very far into the exhibit, you may find it easier to get back to *GNN* using the **GNN** menu.

If you do back up all the way to the last document you saw in *GNN*, you will return to the listing of Art resources. At this point, you can choose to visit other servers on the list. One that is very different, and definitely not classical, is OTIS, which stands for Operative Term Is Stimulate. See what today's artists are creating using all kinds of computer-based tools.

Or, if you want to choose a different subject, scroll to the bottom of the Art listings and find the navigational icon for *The Whole Internet Catalog*. If you click on it, you will go back to the *Catalog*'s front page, where the subject listings are found.

U.S. Department of Education

Let's choose another subject area—Government. Select the link for Government, then find the list for U.S. Government Agencies. On that list, you will find the U.S. Department of Education; click on that link.

As the description says, this is an information server that provides all kinds of documents generated by the U.S. Department of Education (**ed.gov**). This entry also includes **GO** links to their Web, Gopher, and FTP servers. We will explain how to use Gopher and FTP in Chapter 4, *Accessing Other Internet Services*; however, when given the choice among servers (presuming that you are using Mosaic), always choose the Web server. If you do so, you will go to this Web server's home page, as shown in Figure 3-7. This server is fairly straightforward; it contains a listing of its contents, most of which are presented on this same page. In other words, if you click on the link near the beginning of the Contents list, you will go to a location further down in the same document. (Mosaic doesn't retrieve the document again off the Net.) This is a form of "outlining" the contents of a document using links. In long documents, it is useful to have an outline with links to the various parts of the document below. Such a list is often labeled "Contents," but another way to identify one is that the links will be displayed as though you had visited them (typically, dashed underline instead of a solid underline) because their destinations appear in the same document.

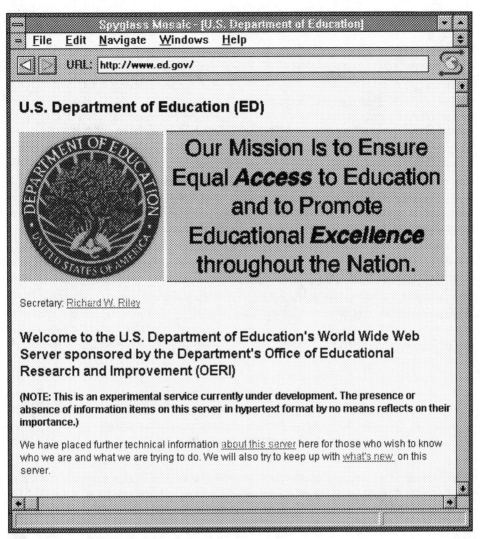

Figure 3-7. Department of Education Web server

Continue, if you wish, to explore the contents of this server. Otherwise, back up to *The Whole Internet Catalog.*

The Paleontology Server

Let's find one more resource in a different subject area—Science. Click on the link for Science and you will see a list of additional categories, one for each discipline. Use the scroll bar to move down through the list and find Paleontology. If you select this link, you will see a list of servers on Paleontology, such as:

```
Honolulu Community College Dinosaur Exhibit
U.C. Berkeley Museum of Paleontology Gopher
U.C. Berkeley Museum of Paleontology Public Exhibits
Paleontological Society Gopher
Palynology & Palaeoclimatology (ANU Bioinformatics Hypermedia Service)
```

Choosing the U.C. Berkeley Museum of Paleontology Public Exhibits link will take you to an entry for this server; select the **GO** link to visit it. This particular server has a well-defined but rather large graphic interface.

Once again, you have ventured to a new server and you can explore it as you wish. If you find the Paleontology server interesting, you may want to add it to your hotlist, so that you can go back to it easily. A good way to use the *Catalog* is to find servers and then compile your own list of those you'd like to visit on a regular basis.

Alternative views of the Catalog

If you return to *The Whole Internet Catalog* front page, you will find several alternative ways to find information in the *Catalog*. You can look at the following:

Top 50
:   This document is a list of the entries most frequently accessed in *The Whole Internet Catalog*. It represents what users find most interesting in the *Catalog*.

    For instance, you might use the list to check out some of the most popular servers. One server that tends to stay high up on the charts is the Web server for Recipe Archives. You can search the recipe archives when you are at work and you can't consult *The Joy of Cooking*.

What's New
:   This document describes the most recent updates to the *Catalog*, listing new information servers or ones that have been removed for some reason.

Searching
:   As of this edition, the searching is somewhat limited. (We are working on improving it.) You can search using the search dialog box at the bottom of each document; however, that currently searches all of *GNN*, not just the *Catalog*. Searching does not currently work on all *GNN* servers.

An alternative is to browse a list of servers by name. Click on the link for "All Catalog Entries" and you will get an alphabetical listing of all the information servers indexed in the *Catalog*. If you select **Find** from the **Edit** menu, you can search this document, and perhaps find a server of interest.

Mosaic Handbook Hotlist

We have created a special list of additional resources that you can use to explore the Net and organized them as the *Mosaic Handbook Hotlist*. This *Hotlist* is on the *GNN* server, and there is a link to it on the Home Page. Choose the link **Chapter 3, Exploring the Web**, to get a list of pointers to the servers that we describe in the rest of this chapter. (This will save you having to type in the URLs to access them.) Many of the services can be found in *The Whole Internet Catalog* as well.

It is always possible that these URLs may change, so be sure to check the links on the *Mosaic Handbook Hotlist*.

NCSA Mosaic What's New

The NCSA Mosaic *What's New* page is the best place on the Internet to find out about new information servers. This page is updated several times a week, and checking it regularly will help you keep up with developments on the Web. Its URL is *http://www.ncsa.uiuc.edu/SDG/Software/Mosaic/Docs/whats-new.html*. A sample entry from this page is shown below:

Labyrinth Electronic Publishing Project
Indiana University, Bloomington, Indiana
> The Honors Division at Indiana University is proud to announce the unveiling of the Labyrinth Electronic Publishing Project, including: collections of poetry from IU faculty and students, and collections of visual art. Take a look and leave some comments on the art and poetry, or if you are feeling creative yourself, leave some noise on the Graffiti Wall.

What's New announcements are organized by date and presented as short descriptions of new resources or Net happenings. Each announcement contains links to the sites being described.

There is also a What's New archive going back to June 1993. Of course, some of this information can be dated and not as useful, but you can often use it to check for a particular site.

The What's New page is often good reading simply because of the variety in the announcements from educational, government, and commercial sites.

FAQ Directory

Frequently Asked Questions (FAQs) are lists of questions that new users often ask, in particular, users of USENET newsgroups. As new users visit a newsgroup, they begin asking questions, and many of these questions have been asked by others before them. Eventually, someone realizes that he or she has answered "newbie" questions often enough and sets about creating a document that compiles these questions and their answers.

Don't get the idea that FAQs are simply answers to obvious questions; they represent the collective wisdom of the Net, and their authors take their work very seriously. You can almost regard the collection of FAQs as an online encyclopedia, they are that broad. By no means are they limited to computer or Internet-related topics. Are you interested in Games or Greek culture, Hockey or Hong Kong, Magic, Model Railroads, or Mexico? All have FAQs.

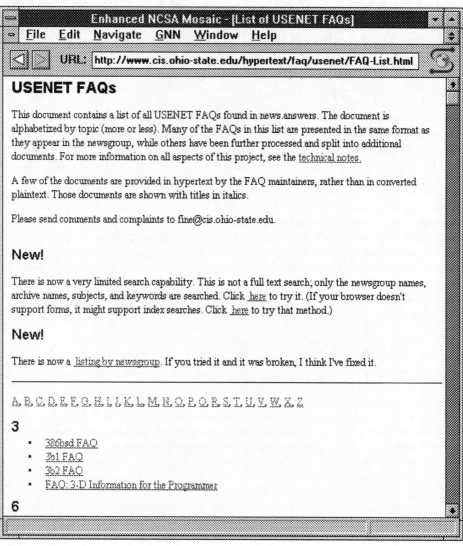

Figure 3-8. USENET FAQs

There's another reason that the FAQ Directory is like an encyclopedia. You might go there looking for one thing and find yourself browsing any number of subjects that you may know nothing about. That's probably true of a lot of Web servers, which is what makes exploring the Web so enjoyable. Figure 3-8 shows the opening page for USENET FAQs, found on the Ohio State University server and compiled by Thomas Fine. Its URL is *http://www.cis.ohio-state.edu/hypertext/faq/usenet /FAQ-List.html*. You might use this directory of FAQs to find subjects that interest you and learn about a newsgroup where people discuss that subject.

The first thing you should do is scroll down the page, where you will begin to see the long alphabetical list of FAQ subjects. When you select an item on the list, you get one of the following:

- a full FAQ in ASCII text

- a list of questions, shown as hypertext links that you can follow to get the answer

- a list containing several FAQs on a subject, or parts of a single FAQ

For example, if you select "European Union" from the list, you will get a single ASCII document that explains the charter of the European Union and answers basic questions about its objectives.

If you select the Dogs FAQ, you get a list of FAQs on subjects ranging from obedience training to health. There are even more FAQs available on the next level, covering different breeds.

The FAQ server is beginning to offer different ways to access its documents. A new search facility is in the experimental stages so that you can search for an FAQ without knowing its main subject title.

Netizens

Getting to know others like yourself who are exploring the Internet can be fun. You may know people from email or from their postings in newsgroups. However, the Web has encouraged new forms of expression and users are taking advantage of it by creating their own home pages and putting them on the Net.

GNN has a publication called *Netizens* in which users list their home pages for others to view. Visit *Netizens* and see who else is out there on the Internet. Its URL is *http://gnn.com/gnn/meta/internet/netizens/*. From the *Netizens* front page, shown in Figure 3-9, you can browse an alphabetical listing of names or a listing of the most recent additions. For each user, you will find an email address, a location, and a mention of their interests. Most have supplied a link to a home page on their own server.

After you've read Chapter 7, *Creating HTML Documents*, which describes how to create your own home page in HTML, come back and add your name and become a Netizen.

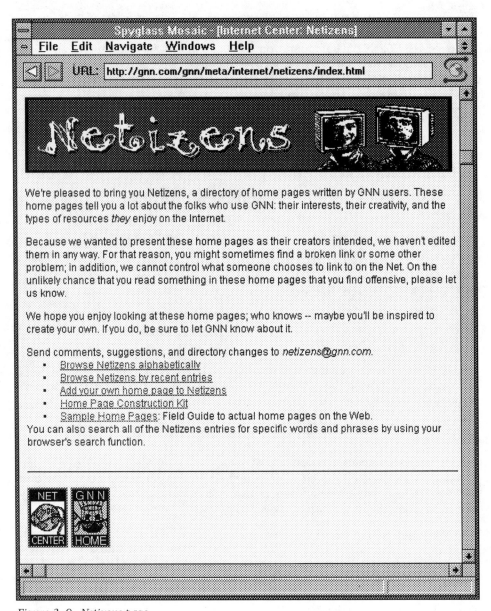

Figure 3–9. Netizens page

Commercial Sites on the Web

If you'd like to know if a particular business has information available on the World Wide Web, the Commercial Sites on the Web server at MIT is a good place to look. This student-run server offers an alphabetical listing of companies by name, which are linked directly to their sites. Its URL is *http://tns-www.lcs.mit.edu /commerce.html*. The current document lists over 300 commercial sites, which is one sign of the increasing business activity on the Net. For instance, if you'd like to find out if your favorite computer company is on the Net and offers support, look them up on this server. Remember that this server is essentially just a listing of links to other servers.

If you can't find a particular company, you may know its domain name by exchanging email with someone in that organization. The domain name for O'Reilly & Associates is **ora.com**; for IBM, it is **ibm.com**. If a company has a Web server, it often can be reached by composing an HTTP URL that prefixes "www" to the domain name. For instance, *http://www.ibm.com/*. It may also work without the "www" prefix. Either way, we are guessing at the URL based on conventional practice, but this syntax is not enforced by any software. It produces an error if the company does not have a server or if the server resides at a different address.

GNN also provides several ways for you to find companies that want to deliver information about products and services to Mosaic users. The *GNN Business Listings* are advertiser-paid listings that describe in brief what a company does and what information it provides online. This information is provided in a consistent format for users. You can search companies by product or service category as well as by name.

Discovering Information Services

This section gives an overview of different kinds of Web-based information services. We look at online exhibits, magazines, international kiosks, and interactive media centers.

The servers listed in this section can be accessed directly from the *Mosaic Handbook Hotlist*, but their URLs are also listed here.

Exhibits

An online exhibit organizes a collection of materials for easy access. Usually, an exhibit integrates text and graphics as a series of documents. Exhibits are usually created by universities or museums, and the number is increasing daily.

- Artserve
  http://rubens.anu.edu.au/

Artserve from Professor Michael Greenhalgh of Australian National University is a collection of digitized art organized as an art history database. Professor Greenhalgh is also responsible for the Palace at Split that we demonstrated earlier.

- **Vatican Exhibit**
  http://sunsite.unc.edu/expo/vatican.exhibit/Vatican.exhibit.html

The *Vatican Library MSS Exhibit*, which can be found in the Art section of the *Catalog*, is a guided tour through the collections of the Vatican Library, as they were showcased at the Library of Congress. This exhibit includes some exceptionally beautiful illuminated manuscripts, which are presented as postage-stamp sized images that you can click on to retrieve an enlarged image in a separate window.

- **Dead Sea Scrolls**
  http://sunsite.unc.edu/expo/deadsea.scrolls.exhibit/intro.html

Another interesting exhibition from the Library of Congress is the *Scrolls from the Dead Sea*. This exhibit can be found in Archaeology section of the *Catalog*.

- **Hubble Space Telescope**
  http://stsci.edu/top.html

A fascinating scientific exhibit is sponsored by the *Space Telescope Science Institute* at Johns Hopkins University in Baltimore, Maryland. This resource can be found in the Astronomy section of the *Catalog*. Its home page is shown in Figure 3-9. It includes information about the Hubble Space Telescope as well as a collection of images, including some from the Shoemaker-Levy comet that impacted Jupiter in July of 1994. There are a number of collections of interest to educators and the naturally curious, including a digitized sky survey.

Magazines

When *GNN* premiered in the fall of 1993, we were the first to create a commercial Web-based magazine. Our first issue of *GNN Magazine* was about the U.S. Government's role in developing the Internet and its involvement in making more information available to the public. Our second issue was on education, and we showed many examples of how teachers are using the Internet in the classroom. Now, *GNN* has developed special-interest magazines in Travel and Personal Finance, with more to come soon.

Creating a magazine can involve more than putting the text of an article online (the most common approach used for a magazine that originates in print). Of particular interest are online magazines that utilize the medium most effectively to create and present content. The Web will be a fascinating place for large and small publishers to create all kinds of magazines, perhaps reaching even more specialized audiences. In a few years the Internet will have more magazines than your local newsstand. Here are some examples you can find today.

- **International Teletimes**
  http://www.wimsey.com/teletimes.root/teletimes_home_page.html

International Teletimes is published in Vancouver, British Columbia, as a general-interest magazine. It is representative of many new magazines that are original to the Internet and have no print counterpart. Some are more sophisticated than

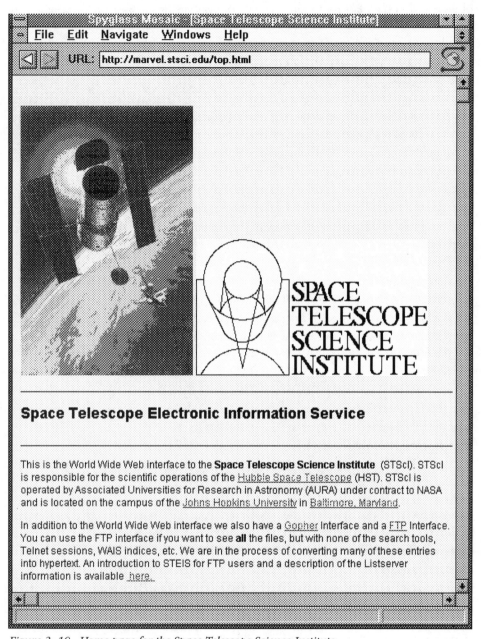

Figure 3–10. Home page for the Space Telescope Science Institute

others, and you'll also find that many of the online magazines or *'zines* are very personal in nature, and can be narrowly focused or broadly defined.

- **Zines**
  http://www.ora.com:8080/johnl/e-zine-list/

GNN Technical Services Manager John Labovitz maintains a 'zines list. This is a reasonably comprehensive list of electronic magazines published on the Net. Many of the 'zines are ASCII-text only, but there are a wide range of formats. Editorially, they are usually idiosyncratic, rather like fanzines and underground newspapers.

- **Wired**
  http://www.wired.com/

Wired is a magazine oriented toward technology and culture, with an attitude. Its Web server contains sample articles and other information. If you enjoy *Wired*, but find its page layout distracting, reading it online can be a much more pleasant experience. They have announced plans to create a *HotWired* online service based on Web technology.

- **Mother Jones**
  http://www.mojones.com/motherjones.html

Mother Jones, the mother of investigative reporting, has a Web server at **mojones.com**. You will find a cover image and articles for its bimonthly issues. A sample article from the July/August 1994 issue is "The Cry of the Ocean," by Peter Steinhart, which leads off a special report on how the world fish population is depleted and the consequences not only for the fishing industry but for all of us. The special report ends with an article, "Fishing in the Net," that suggests a few places on the Internet where you can find related information.

International kiosks

International kiosks provide information about individual countries or states. The Regional and Cultural Interest section of *The Whole Internet Catalog* contains pointers to most countries. Some of these servers use only the native language of the country (i.e., the Norway server is in Norwegian), while others have materials in English as well. For more information on particular countries, check the listing of servers by country described later in this chapter.

- **New Zealand**
  http://www.cs.cmu.edu:8001/Web/People/mjw/NZ/MainPage.html

The *New Zealand Information* server, by Michael Witbrock, is a Best of the Net selection. This server is not located in New Zealand, though, but at Carnegie-Mellon University. Even so, it has a lot of depth in its information, and many unusual items.

- **Japan**
  http://www.ntt.jp/japan/

You can learn more about Japan on a *Japanese Information* Web server sponsored by Nippon Telephone and Telegraph (NTT) and produced by Takada Toshihiro. You can find Japanese-language documents as well as a traveler's guide to speaking Japanese, which includes audio samples. You can hear the Japanese national anthem, *Kimigayo*, played on a recorder. You can also find a map of Japan, as well as a lot of political and cultural information.

- **Iceland**
  http://www.rfisk.is/english/iceland/rest_of_iceland.html

You can take a tour of Iceland; if you click on a map of Iceland you'll get photographs from a specific city or region.

- **Germany**
  http://www.chemie.fu-berlin.de/adressen/brd.html

Get more familiar with Germany online. This server contains geopolitical information, as well as a map of Germany. It also provides access to a German language news service.

Interactive media centers

All Web servers can be considered interactive because of the nature of hypertext. You choose what interests you and go in that direction, almost instantly. However, a number of servers have created special interactive interfaces.

- **Xerox PARC Map Viewer**
  http://pubweb.parc.xerox.com/map

The *Xerox PARC Map Viewer* is a Best of the Net selection that allows you to generate maps of specific areas that you select.

- **United States Map**
  http://ageninfo.tamu.edu/apl-us/

The *Digital Relief Map of the United States* is a color relief map composed of cells. If you click on a cell, Mosaic retrieves a full-blown image of that cell. The map was created by Ray Sterner of the Applied Physics Laboratory at Johns Hopkins University, and distributed on the Web by Hal Mueller of Texas A&M University. This server can be accessed from the Geography section of the *Catalog*.

- **The Geometry Center**
  http://www.geom.umn.edu/welcome.html

The Geometry Center at the University of Minnesota, which is dedicated to "the computation and visualization of geometric structures," says that part of its mission is to help mathematicians reach the public. You will find an interesting picture archive, forums, and software, some of which only run on workstations. Be sure to check out "A Gallery of Interactive On-Line Geometry."

- **Exploratorium**
  http://www.exploratorium.edu/

San Francisco's innovative Exploratorium has a Web server called *ExploraNet* that is worth looking at. This hands-on science museum is taking advantage of the Net to create an interactive learning center for kids and adults.

Other Lists and Resource Guides

In addition to *GNN*'s *The Whole Internet Catalog*, there are many subject-oriented lists and resource guides. These lists vary in completeness and timeliness. Some are organized well; others require you to scroll doggedly down a long screen (or screen after screen) of alphabetized entries.

In this section, we describe a sampling of lists and guides that you might find useful.

CERN's General Overview of the Web

Overview: *http://info.cern.ch/hypertext/WWW/LineMode/Defaults/default.html*
Virtual Library: *http://info.cern.ch/hypertext/DataSources/bySubject/Overview.html*
Servers by Country: *http://info.cern.ch/hypertext/DataSources/WWW/Geographical.html*

The *General Overview of the Web* at CERN is a comprehensive, though less user-friendly, picture of what's available on the Web. On its "Overview" home page, it says that there is no "top" to the Web. This becomes immediately apparent when you link to the *Virtual Library*, which is a distributed subject catalog arranged alphabetically. There is no description of any of the resources in the list; instead, there is just a straight link out to the resource, so it's hard to know what to expect until you get there.

What this listing lacks in descriptiveness it makes up for in comprehensiveness. From Aeronautics and Aeronautical Engineering to Sports, pick a subject you're interested in and click on the link. What you'll get is another list of resources that relate to that subject. These lists are not arranged alphabetically; sometimes there's a brief description of the resource, sometimes there isn't.

If you're looking for information on a specific subject, you'll have to sift through a number of entries on this page before you find a link to what you're looking for—and you may *not* find such a link!

As with NCSA Mosaic's *What's New* page, the *Virtual Library* page gets a lot of its information on new resources from readers who submit pointers to these resources. The *Virtual Library* encourages readers to submit these pointers to maintainers, each of whom is responsible for a particular subject area. Updates appear to be fairly frequent.

Also available on the *General Overview of the Web* page is a list of servers, which lists all registered Web servers by country. When you click on this link, you'll see links to registered WWW servers organized by continent, country, and state. It is a long, exhaustive list, and it does contain some explanatory text for some of the entries. It's a great resource if you want to know more about a particular country, especially if you wish to find information in a foreign language.

Figure 3-11 shows the page that lists Web servers by country. Scroll down the list until you see South America (doing so will demonstrate that North America is most heavily represented). Click on the link for Peru. You will go to a brief description of Red Cientifica Peruana, the Internet Network of Peru. You can follow a link to their server in Peru. Offered in Spanish and (some) English, this server gives basic information about the country, and links to Latin American and Caribbean Gopher servers.

Because this list is so extensive, you might want to use the **Find** feature in Mosaic to locate a particular country or state rather than scroll through the list.

To give you an example of how you can use this list as a point of departure for what can be a fascinating trip to almost anywhere in the world, follow the sequence of links below:

1. Find Malaysia on the list of Web servers by country and follow that link.

2. On the next document, follow the link to the University Sains Malaysia (USM) at Penang server.

3. On the USM server, follow the link to Penang Island.

This document is a tourist information guide, describing the geography, history, and climate of the area. It lists its contents as links at the top. If you select the **Local Food** link you can read about various local dishes, including murtabak: "An Indian styled pizza filled with all the goodness of minced meat and onions and fried over a hot plate. It is eaten with a vegetarian curry."

CERN's list of servers gives you an appreciation of how big the Web really is.

Special Internet Connections

http://info.cern.ch/hypertext/DataSources/Yanoff.html

Scott Yanoff offers a standard list of Internet services, which he began compiling in 1991. This exhaustive list, which is organized under broad categories such as Aviation, Law, and Travel (arranged alphabetically), contains entries and links to any kind of Internet service you can think of, from Gopher to TELNET, and everything in between. Though lengthy, the list is made up of terse entries that are not particularly descriptive of the resources they are pointing to. It is not updated on a regular schedule.

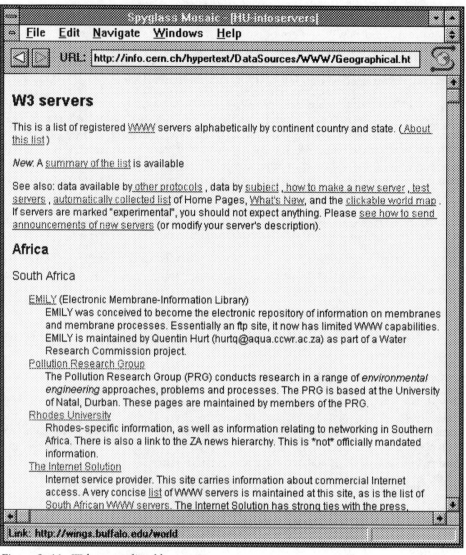

Figure 3–11. Web servers listed by country

CyberSight

http://cybersight.com/cgi-bin/cs/s?main.gmml

Terse is not the word to describe CyberSight, however. Billed as the central online "jumping off" point for alternative information seekers, CyberSight offers links to off-beat resources in a lively format. Don't approach this server with any preconceptions; just go to "The What You Want List (nutritious too!)" and choose from a few of the eclectic categories (Hot Stuff, Kitsch, Cybversive). For example, if you go to the Funky category, you'll see pointers to such unusual resources as "Coke Machines," a site that helps you track the status of Coke and other vending machines around the world. Another site, "Roadkill R Us" ("a cornucopia of carcasses"), will give you access to more information on the truly tasteless than you ever dreamed of finding.

Searching the Web

After you've used these lists, you might decide to set out on your own to find things on the Web. You'll find several useful databases (or automated indexes), with new ones appearing all the time. Not all the searching interfaces are easy to use, and some searches will result in dead-ends or direct you to more information than you want.

The first thing to know about searching on the Web is that you are not really searching the documents on the Web itself. Rather, you are searching databases of information that have been collected from documents on the Web. These databases may include information for each document such as:

- Title

- Location (the URL)

- Documents that are linked to and from this document

- Keywords, abstracts, or brief descriptions of document contents

All this data is gathered off the Net and organized into a database, with links pointing back to the original documents. When you search for a word or phrase, you are really running a program on a remote computer that knows how to query and extract information from these databases. If your search is successful (i.e., your search words match up with words in the database), the program on the remote computer returns a Web document that contains links to the original documents.

Many of the searching databases are constructed and updated by programs called "robots" or "spiders" that continually "travel" the Net finding documents. As they encounter documents, they record information about each document, which is then used to update the database of documents.

Although robots sound like the perfect way to search the Web, there are a few problems. First, it takes a long time to search the Web, and so databases generated by robots may become out of date as documents are deleted or moved. Second, robots are generally indiscriminate about what databases they search, and a search in a robot-generated database may result in a huge number of "successful" searches, but a small number of really useful documents.

NOTE

For information on the general design of robots, and technical descriptions of robot programs on the Web, see "World Wide Web Wanderers, Spiders and Robots" (*http://web.nexor.co.uk/mak/doc/robots/robots.html*).

Most searching interfaces have a single text entry field for entering simple queries. Some interfaces are more complex, allowing you to reduce the scope of your search. Unless otherwise specified, most searchers will find any instance of a word, whether full or partial, upper- or lowercase. For example, entering "zine" will match "magazine" as well as "zine." Below we introduce a number of these search servers for the Web.

The Wanderer

http://www.mit.edu:8001/people/mkgray/comprehensive.html

If at this point you're asking the question, "How big is the Web?" go to The World Wide Web Wanderer, a Perl script automaton created by Matthew Grey. The Wanderer travels the Web searching for Web sites. It does a breadth-first search of the Web, looking for and including in a queue all the URLs contained in every document it encounters. At last count (June 1994), the Wanderer had found more than 3000 sites on the Web. These are all listed (by numerical IP addresses, host sites, or by country); check out part or all of the list to see just how big your search can be when you search the Web.

CUSI

http://web.nexor.co.uk/susi/cusi.html

CUSI, part of the Web at Nexor (a UK-based technology company) is a forms-based interface to many of the searchable indexes listed below, as well as other databases including catalogs, phone books, dictionaries, and technical documents. It's relatively easy to use, and you'll find it helpful to have so many of these searchers available in one document.

ALIWEB

http://web.nexor.co.uk/aliweb/doc/aliweb.html

ALIWEB (Archie-Like Indexing for the Web) is a distributed indexing system. Because it is modeled after Archie, a program that maintains a database of software programs listed in public archives on the Net, you ask it where to find a particular program. ALIWEB's index database is generated from descriptions stored as files on the servers that contain the documents being indexed. This means that as long as publishers keep their own local descriptions up to date, ALIWEB has the potential to be of high quality. However, because it doesn't index every document on the Web, it's not a good place to look for instances of specific words or phrases.

CUI W3 Catalog

http://cui_www.unige.ch/w3catalog

The CUI searcher is a database of indexes to several popular lists and resource guides, including:

- NCSA's What's New

- NCSA's Starting Points

- CERN's W3 Virtual Library Subject Catalog and selected sub-lists

- Martijn Koster's ALIWEB—Archie-like Indexing for the Web

- Scott Yanoff's Internet Services List

- Simon Gibbs' list of Multimedia Information Sources

- John December's list of Computer-Mediated Communication Information Sources and Internet Tools Summary

Most of these resources are manually maintained subject-oriented lists (some of which are described earlier in this chapter), making the CUI catalog a good place to start if you know the topic of a search ("agriculture," for instance). Also, if a search is successful, it will return not just a list of documents, but the entry that contains the word or phrase.

WebCrawler

http://www.biotech.washington.edu/WebCrawler/WebQuery.html

WebCrawler is a robot that keeps an index of the contents of all the documents it comes across. Its interface is surprisingly simple—you type the words you're looking for into a single text entry box and click **Search**. A checkbox controls whether the words you are looking for must all be present in a document being searched (logical "AND") or whether only a subset may be present (logical "OR").

EINet Galaxy

http://www.einet.net/galaxy.html

EINet Galaxy is a combination hierarchical subject catalog and searchable database. This server, unlike the others, grabs all the documents it can find (not just HTML) and indexes them in a WAIS server. Thus you are searching the content of the Web and you get back as many hits as you ask for. It has a confusing interface, however, and searches often result in a large number of items returned.

The World Wide Web Worm

http://www.cs.colorado.edu/home/mcbryan/WWWW.html

The World Wide Web Worm is a database of Web document titles, URLs, and cross-references. Its power lies in the detailed level of searching that can be done: in addition to searching for words or phrases in a document title, you can search for specific URLs or patterns within URLs. For instance, you can find documents at a particular host by searching for the hostname in the URL database. You can even search for particular types of files—searching for ".mpg" might find all the MPEG moving-image files in the database. Because WWWW keeps track of links between documents, you can supply a URL and find all the documents that link to that URL. The WWWW home page describes many such powerful search examples, although it doesn't say how often the Worm does its work.

Before concluding this tour of the Web, we should add that you are exploring an ever-expanding online universe. Things change every day, at every hour. This is especially important to remember if you can't find what you are looking for, or if the subject area of key interest does not have a strong set of resources on the Net. Someone may notice the deficiency one day and begin putting up a lot of useful information the next day. You may even be the person who makes that contribution!

CHAPTER FOUR

ACCESSING OTHER INTERNET SERVICES

Mosaic and Gopher
WAIS
Mosaic and FTP
Network News

S o far, we have used Mosaic to access Web servers. However, Mosaic can also access other types of Internet servers, such as Gopher, WAIS, and FTP. In Chapter 1, *The Wide World of Internet Services*, we explained that these services were available on the Internet before Web servers existed. Each service has its own distinct way of providing information to users, just as the Web does. However, Mosaic can be used not only as a Web client, but also as a Gopher client. It can be used as a client to access WAIS servers, news servers, and FTP archives. Because Mosaic is such a multipurpose browser, it has become the Swiss Army knife of the Internet.

In exploring the Internet, you may be surprised when you traverse a link and you don't end up in a Web document. Instead, you'll see a list of topics, each one appearing as a link, and, if you look at the URL, you will be able to identify it as a Gopher server. Similarly, you may see a list of filenames and directories. If you check the URL, you'll find that you have accessed an FTP server. In both cases, it is pretty obvious that you are not viewing a Web document.

In this chapter, we demonstrate how to use Mosaic to access these different types of servers. You don't have to learn too much about navigating to these servers. Rather, you will come to recognize the differences in the way they organize information. Knowing that a link points to a Gopher server tells you something about how the information will be presented.

Below is a list of the services covered in this chapter, along with a short description of each.

Gopher   Gopher is a menu-based information system that allows users to browse through a hierarchical organization and select items from menus. Each item on the menu represents either a file or a directory.

WAIS   WAIS, which stands for Wide Area Information Servers, is a search-and-retrieval system that lets users search a full-text index of all documents in a database.

FTP   FTP, which stands for File Transfer Protocol, is an application that lets you download files from remote servers.

Network news   Network news is a system of bulletin board discussion groups covering every kind of subject from computer science to sex, pets, and surfboarding.

If you are interested in learning more about the Internet services discussed in this chapter and comparing other client interfaces, see *The Whole Internet User's Guide and Catalog* by Ed Krol.

Mosaic and Gopher

Not too long ago there were a lot more Gopher servers on the Net than Web servers. There are still a lot of Gopher servers around because they are an easy way to provide information to a broad audience. What is distinctive about Gopher is that you navigate through menus, and each item on the menu is either a file or another menu with additional selections. In Mosaic, these choices are links, and you select the item you want by clicking on the link. Figure 4-1 shows the Library of Congress Gopher as viewed in Mosaic. We begin at the top-level menu of this

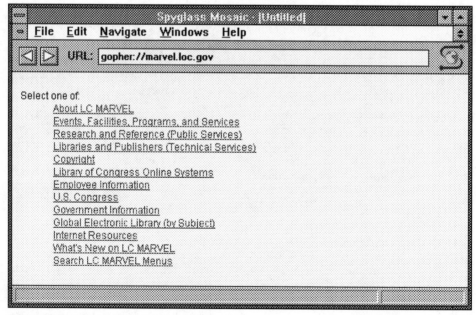

Figure 4-1. Library of Congress Gopher

Gopher. If you click on **Government Information**, Mosaic retrieves the contents of that menu, as shown in Figure 4-2.

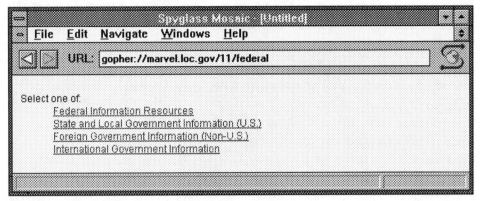

Figure 4–2. Government Information menu

This menu contains four links, each of which takes you to another menu as you navigate to the next level of detail in the hierarchy. Clicking on **Federal Information Resources** takes you to a menu with more directories. On you go, tunneling through directories until you come to a menu that contains some files. Clicking on a filename displays the contents of the file. Most Gopher servers deliver ASCII files that Mosaic displays in a fixed font. An example of such a file is shown in Figure 4-3. Besides letting users browse through categories of information, Gopher can transparently access information from other Gopher servers. In addition, most Gopher servers contain pointers to all the other Gopher servers in the world, so it is truly a global system.

There are some disadvantages, however. In our example, we didn't go through all the layers of menus that it took to get to a text file, but there were more than a dozen. Sometimes Gopher seems like a case study in the limitations of hierarchical filing systems. The problem is that it becomes absurd (not to mention boring) to keep selecting menu items, only to be confronted by another menu list. After padding through a dozen or so of these menus, you may lose interest in whatever you were looking for.

Given the choice, most people would rather use a Web server than a Gopher server. However, you don't always have a choice, as some organizations may not yet be able to provide information in HTML on a Web server. You also see interesting Web/Gopher hybrids. For example, if a business already has a Gopher server, they might create a Web server with only a few original documents that serve as a high-level interface to the Gopher server. In other words, after the home page, their Web server points to information managed on the Gopher server.

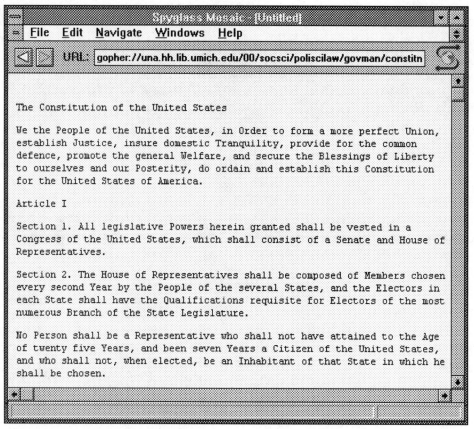

Figure 4-3. Mosaic displays an ASCII file

That said, however, remember that lots of good information can be found in Gopher servers. *The Whole Internet Catalog* in *GNN* contains pointers to quite a few good Gopher servers, including:

- African National Congress Gopher

- The Bible

- Envirogopher

- CIA World Factbook

- Project Gutenberg

- The California Museum of Photography

Using the Hotlist to Manage Gophers

Since the good stuff (the documents) may be buried several layers deep in a Gopher, you'll want to use all the tools at your disposal to manage them. You can use your hotlist to create bookmarks in the Gophers you use regularly. Each menu level in Gopher can be identified by a URL. Thus, when you get to the menu level that you want, you can just choose **Add This Document** from the **Navigate** menu to add that Gopher menu to your hotlist. Of course, you can still travel up and down the menus once you're in the Gopher.

Getting Gophers with URLs

A Gopher URL is a lot like a Web URL, except that the service protocol is different, of course. Instead of *http*, you use the Gopher protocol. So to contact the Library of Congress Gopher, select **Open URL** from the **File** menu and type:

```
gopher://marvel.loc.gov
```

This takes you to the main menu of the server. As discussed above, it becomes pure drudgery to have to navigate through all those menus. Mosaic can help you avoid some of this awkwardness by allowing you to connect directly to a particular menu level. For instance, you can get directly to the **Federal Information Resources** menu in the Library of Congress Gopher by typing the URL:

```
gopher://marvel.loc.gov/11/federal/fedinfo
```

Searching Through Gopherspace

Since tunneling through menus can be a time-consuming way to find information, especially if you're looking for specific information, there are several applications for searching "gopherspace." On a Gopher menu you may see an option for searching. If you select this option, you will go to another document where you are prompted to enter a search keyword. The Gopher server then returns a menu of items matching the search criteria. Many Gopher servers also have a gateway to a WAIS server that contains a full-text index of the contents of the Gopher. We'll talk more about WAIS servers in the next section.

There are also several tools that index all of gopherspace, not just a single server. You can specify a search string that will be matched against an index of words in Gopher titles or text files. Because they are modeled after an Internet search tool called Archie, these search tools were named after characters from the *Archie* comic books.

Veronica

Veronica searches all of the menu items on all Gopher servers for a string of words or characters that you enter. Follow these steps to use Veronica:

1. Log on to the Gopher server at the University of Texas at Austin by entering the following URL:

   ```
   gopher://bongo.cc.utexas.edu
   ```

   Figure 4-4 shows the top-level menu of this Gopher server.

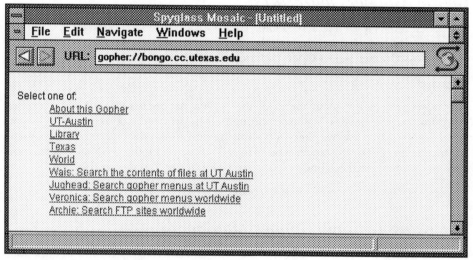

Figure 4-4. Top-level menu of the Gopher server at UT-Austin

2. Select **Veronica: Search Gopher Menus Worldwide**. This leads you to a menu where you can select a Veronica server, shown in Figure 4-5. As you can see, there are actually two types of Veronica searches—you can search the titles of all Gopher items, or you can search only for directories. If you do the first kind of search, you're likely to get a rather long list of results, so doing a directory search is usually more effective.

   There are a number of different servers to choose from. As a general rule, try the server that's closest to you first. Veronica servers tend to be quite busy; you may not be able to access the first server you try. In fact, don't be surprised if you have to go to Europe before you find a server you can access.

3. Assuming you are able to connect, you will then be presented with a screen that contains a text field, shown in Figure 4-6. Simply enter the text you are searching for in the field and press **Return**.

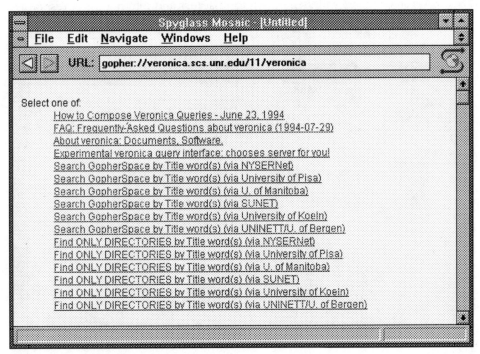

Figure 4–5. Choosing a Veronica server

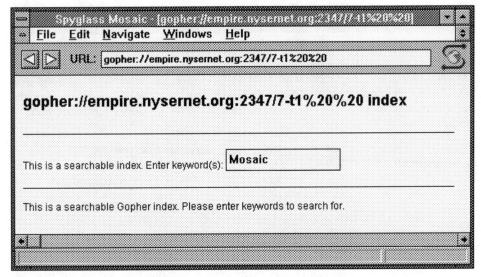

Figure 4–6. Searching Veronica for a string of text

4. The Veronica server will then search for that text and return a list of responses, as shown in Figure 4-7. Each response is a hypertext link, and clicking on one brings up either a menu or the contents of a file.

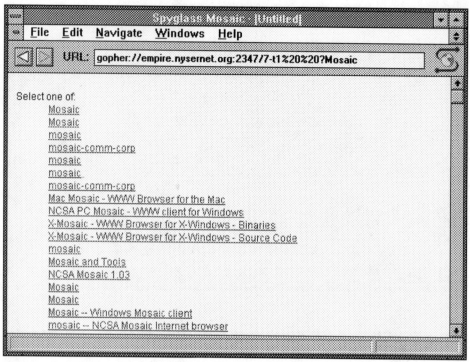

Figure 4-7. Veronica search response

Veronica searches accept "Boolean operators," words that specify conditions that must be met in order for Veronica to consider an item as matching the search. Boolean operators separate two or more strings. Veronica understands the following operators:

- AND tells Veronica that both parts of the query must be present. For instance, searching for "Microsoft AND Windows" tells Veronica that only items that contain both "Microsoft" and "Windows" are matches. If no Boolean operators are specified, Veronica assumes there to be an AND between words.

- OR tells Veronica that either part of the query is acceptable as a match. If the query is "Microsoft OR Windows," any items that contain either one of those words is considered a match.

- NOT tells Veronica to search for items containing the first string but not the second. For instance, searching for "Microsoft NOT Windows" searches for items containing "Microsoft" but excludes items that refer to "Windows" or "Microsoft Windows."

You can combine Boolean operators. Veronica evaluates them from right to left, so "Microsoft AND Windows OR NT" searches for items with "NT" or "Microsoft Windows." Veronica also accepts an asterisk as a wildcard character, which represents any combination of characters to the end of the word. For example, "shovel*" would match shovel, shovels, shoveling, shoveled, and so on.

Jughead

Sometimes you don't want to search the menus of every Gopher server in the world. If you are looking for regional or specialized information, you can use Jughead to search menu titles of Gophers at a single institution. Many colleges and universities use Gopher servers as campus-wide information systems, so students at the University of Texas at Austin can use Jughead to search for information about UTA. Or a medical researcher might use Jughead to search only the Gopher servers at Johns Hopkins University.

In most cases, you use Jughead without knowing it. While UTA's Gopher clearly identifies one menu item as **Jughead: Search Gopher menus at UT Austin**, most others simply say something like **Search Gopher menus at** . . .

As with Veronica, Jughead lets you use the Boolean operators AND, OR, and NOT and the asterisk wildcard. Searches are not case-sensitive. However, Jughead only lets you search for two words at a time and doesn't support the ability to search for specific Gopher resource types.

WAIS

There are approximately 600 WAIS servers on the Internet which let you search the full text of all the documents in a database. You can access WAIS servers through either the Web or Gopher.

To use WAIS within Gopher, you can pick a WAIS server and search for a string of words. Most WAIS servers aren't terribly sophisticated when it comes to advanced searching techniques, so Boolean operators probably won't work. One good thing about WAIS, however, is that you can ask it questions in plain English, like "What information is there about Silicon Graphics, Inc.?"

Here's how to try it out:

1. Connect to the University of Minnesota Gopher at:

   `gopher://gopher.micro.umn.edu`

2. Choose **Other Gopher and Information Servers**.

3. Choose **WAIS-Based Information**.

4. Choose **WAIS Databases by Letter**.

5. At this point, you can either search the directory of WAIS servers or choose from an alphabetical list of servers. Since the names of WAIS databases can be a little strange, it's usually better to search the directory. To do that, choose **Directory of WAIS Databases** and enter your query in the search field. For our example, we'll use the query "health insurance," shown in Figure 4-8.

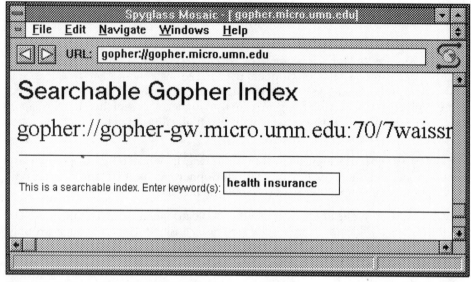

Figure 4–8. Searching the WAIS directory

6. After a little while, Mosaic will display a list of WAIS servers that say they have information about health or insurance, as shown in Figure 4-9.

7. At the top of the list is **Health-Security-Act.src**, which is a database of documents related to the health reform bill proposed by President Clinton in 1994. Click on that link to search the database. Enter your query in the search field, and the server will respond with a ranked list of headlines of documents that contain your search words.

8. To see any of these documents, click on the headline, and Mosaic will display the document. If you want to save it, use the **Save As** command.

You can also use WAIS within certain Web servers. For instance, *The Whole Internet Catalog* includes a WAIS server of the documents in *GNN*. To find documents about finance, you can simply enter "finance" in the search field, and Mosaic will

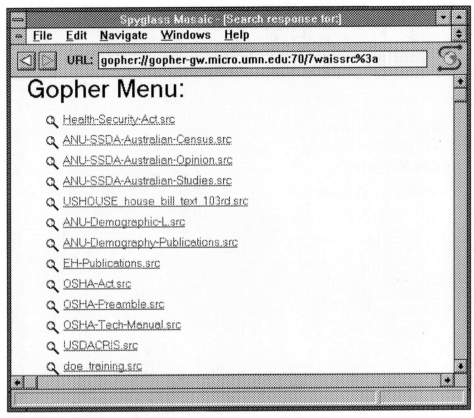

Figure 4–9. Results of WAIS directory search

return a list of description files containing that word, as shown in Figure 4-10. Clicking on one of these files will display the page that contains the link. As of this writing, this feature is only available on *GNN*'s NEARnet server, *http://nearnet.gnn.com/gnn/wic/*.

Mosaic and FTP

Some Web documents, such as *The Whole Internet Catalog*, will link you to FTP servers. FTP is the original Internet application protocol for moving files between computers.

FTP servers generally manage large collections of data—software source code, images, or other data—that is specifically made available for downloading rather than viewing. As a result, files are often stored or compressed in many different formats. This can make FTP a complicated program.

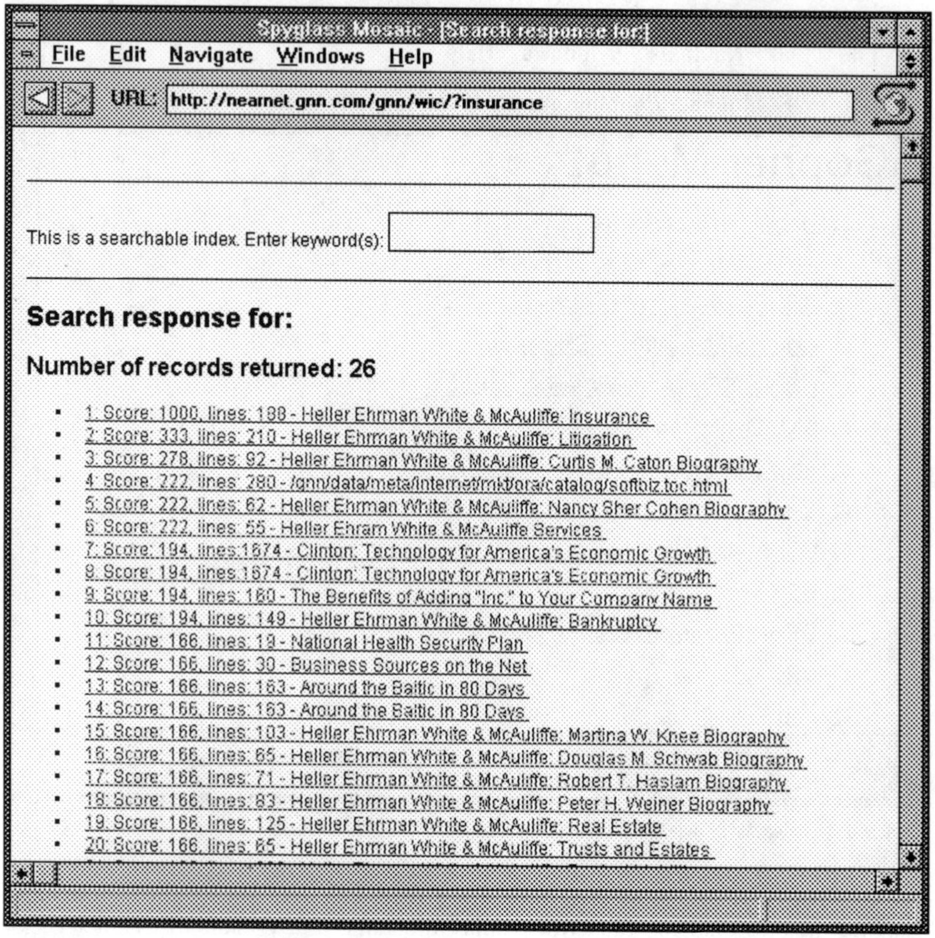

Figure 4–10. Results of searching the WIC

There are two transfer modes available in FTP—one for binary and one for ASCII (text) files. Binary transfer mode preserves the bit sequence of the file, so that the copy is identical to the original. ASCII mode treats the file as sets of characters so that the document will be readable on the computer receiving the file. So, using FTP you would have to specify whether you want a binary or an ASCII transfer.

In addition, files are compressed using many different programs, so it's important to identify which files you can decompress and use on your PC. You can usually determine this by looking at file extensions.

Fortunately, using Mosaic to perform FTP transfers simplifies matters quite a bit. This is because Mosaic determines whether a file should be transferred using ASCII or binary transfer mode.

One important limitation of using Mosaic as an FTP client is that it only supports anonymous FTP, a service that lets you access a public directory via an anonymous login. If you want to transfer files from a computer on which you have an account, you'll need to use another FTP utility.

Downloading Files with FTP

Now let's take a look at using Mosaic to transfer files from an FTP site. We'll start at *The Whole Internet Catalog.* In the Art category, the *WIC* has a link to the Smithsonian Institution's image server **photo1.si.edu**, shown in Figure 4-11. Clicking on the GO button will connect you via anonymous FTP to this server.

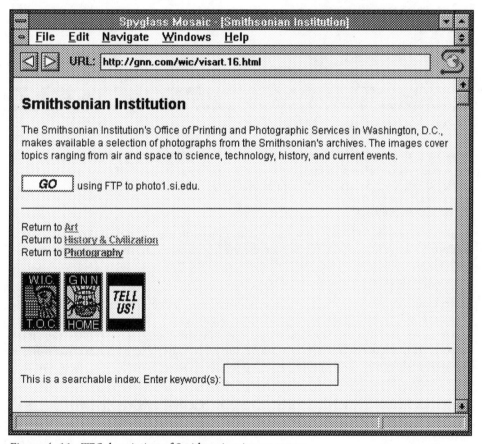

Figure 4–11. WIC description of Smithsonian image server

When you click that button, Mosaic takes care of opening the connection to **photo1.si.edu** and logging you in as an anonymous user. Once connected, Mosaic displays the top-level directories of the server, as shown in Figure 4-12. Now take a look at the URL for this server. The syntax should be familiar to you by now. It

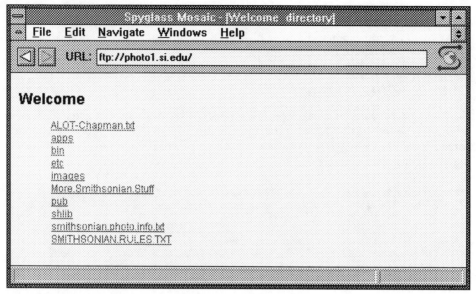

Figure 4-12. Top-level directories of photo1.si.edu

starts with the service protocol *ftp:*, followed by the separator *//* and the name of the server. Directories and filenames can be included in the URL, just as with other services. The URL for the Smithsonian image server, then, is:

```
ftp://photo1.si.edu
```

Unlike in Gopher, FTP directory names are not particularly helpful. Remember that you are looking at a UNIX file server meant for transferring files, not browsing, so hints about content are few and far between. Since this is an image server, though, the *images* directory looks promising.

As you can see, each directory is a hypertext link. Clicking on images will display the contents of that directory, as shown in Figure 4-13. Of the seven items here, two are files and five are subdirectories. The files are the ones with file extensions. Looking at file extensions is pretty much the only way to tell what format a file is in. In this directory, *electronic.times.pdf* is an Adobe Acrobat file, and *smithsonian.photo.info.txt* is a plain text file.

The other items are subdirectories. Three of these—*gif89a*, *jfif-uuencode*, and *jpeg*—look most promising as photo archives since their names contain image file formats.

Before we dive into the image directories, let's take a look at the text file *smithsonian.photo.info.txt* to see what it tells us. To read the file, click on the filename. The file is shown in Figure 4-14.

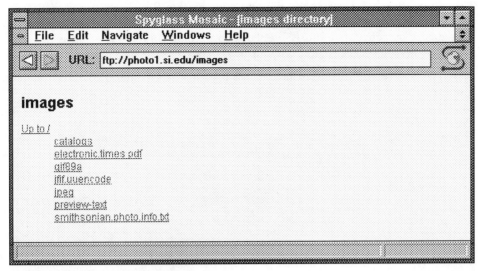

Figure 4-13. The images directory

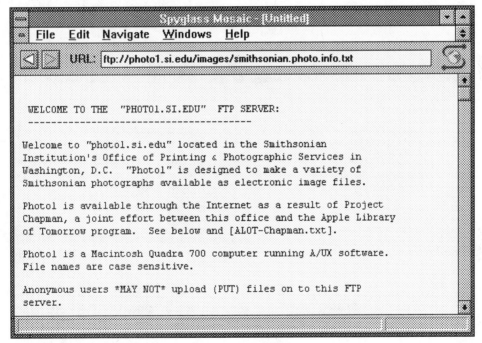

Figure 4-14. Clicking on a text file displays its contents

The information file explains the file and compression formats of the various files and tells us how to download appropriate software for viewing the images. To save this document for future reference, choose **Save As** from the **File** menu and choose a filename and location on your hard disk.

Now let's see what files are available. Click on the **Back** button to return to the directory listing and then click on **gif89a** to see the contents of that directory, as shown in Figure 4-15.

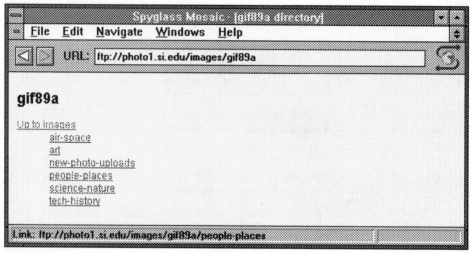

Figure 4-15. Contents of gif89a

The directory contains several subdirectories, which organize the images by category. Let's try the *air-space* directory, shown in Figure 4-16. Finally, we've found the images. Notice that these files all end with the extension *.gif.* That tells us that they're images in the GIF format. Remember, now that you know where you're going, you can get right to this directory by entering the URL:

```
ftp://photo1.si.edu/images/gif89a/air-space
```

Now we're ready to download a file. Let's try APOLLO.GIF. Clicking on the filename brings up the **Save As** dialog box, which, of course, lets you specify where to save the document.

Mosaic asks you to save the document, rather than just display it, because graphics files must be downloaded in binary mode. Mosaic automatically determines whether to transfer in binary or ASCII mode. Table 4-1 shows which mode is used for different file types.

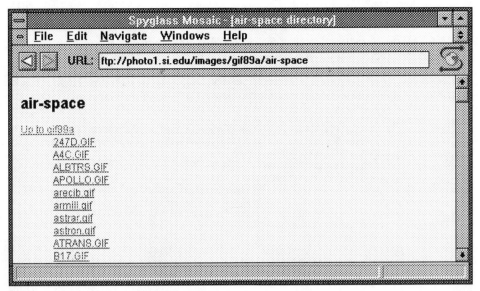

Figure 4–16. Contents of the air-space directory

Table 4–1: Common File Types and Modes

File	Mode
Text file	ASCII, by definition
Spreadsheet	Probably binary
Database file	Probably binary, possibly ASCII
Word processor file	Probably binary, possibly ASCII
Program source code	ASCII
Electronic mail messages	ASCII
UNIX shell archive	ASCII
UNIX tar file	Binary
Backup file	Binary
Compressed file	Binary
Uuencoded or binhexed file	ASCII
Executable file	Binary
PostScript (laser printer) file	ASCII
Hypertext (HTML) document	ASCII
Picture files (GIF, JPEG, MPEG)	Binary

Downloading a Program

When the transfer is complete, you can view the image in any program that can display GIF files. (In Chapter 6, *Using Mosaic for Multimedia*, we'll show you how to view GIF and JPEG images with a program called LView.) If Mosaic is configured to use a GIF viewer, the viewer program will be launched when the download is complete. See Chapter 6 for a detailed discussion of using external viewers with Mosaic. The Smithsonian text file recommended a DOS program called CSHOW, which was located in the *apps* directory. To get this, you can move back up to the main directory by clicking on the **Up to** hypertext, which displays the next highest directory, until you reach the main directory. Then click on **apps**.

The *apps* directory has three subdirectories for DOS, Macintosh, and UNIX. Clicking on **dos** displays the contents of that directory, as shown in Figure 4-17.

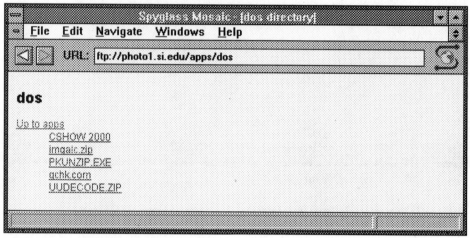

Figure 4-17. Contents of DOS directory

Notice that two of the files in this directory have the extension *.zip*. This indicates that they have been compressed with a DOS compression utility, probably PKZIP. Other times you'll see files with the *.z* or *.gz* extensions. That indicates that a UNIX compression program was used. Table 4-2 gives information about common compression extensions and the associated programs.

Table 4-2: Common Compression Programs

Compression Program	Decompression Program	File Suffix	Typical Filename
compress	uncompress	*.Z*	*rfc1118.txt.Z*
gzip	gunzip	*.z* or *.gz*	*textfile.gz*
pack	unpack	*.z*	*textfile.z*
Stuffit	unsit	*.Sit*	*program.Sit*
PackIt	unpit	*.pit*	*report.pit*
PKZIP	unzip41	*.ZIP*	*package.ZIP*
zoo210	zoo210	*.zoo*	*picture.zoo*

The program we want, however, is in the CSHOW directory. Clicking on it reveals that there are two files in the directory, *cshowa.exe* (the program file) and *describe.txt*. (Files with the *.exe* extension are DOS or Windows application files.)

Click on the text file first to learn about the CSHOW program, then go back and download the program file.

Figure 4-18 shows what APOLLO.GIF looks like.

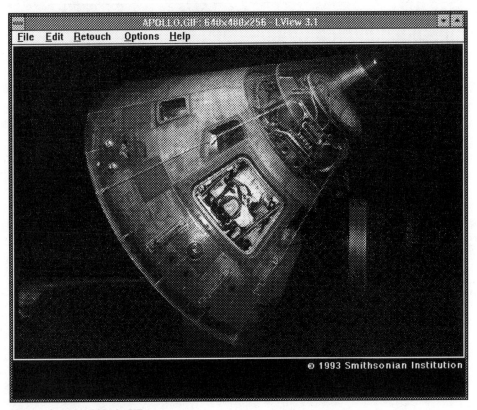

Figure 4–18. APOLLO.GIF

Using FTP with Hypertext

Another way to use FTP in Mosaic is through hypertext links. Some servers, such as the NCSA Web server, let you download specific files via anonymous FTP by clicking on a hypertext link. This is, of course, a very simple way to get files; you don't have to wade through the FTP server—just click on a link and the file transfer process starts transparently.

As an example, try downloading an external viewer from NCSA's WinMosaic page. To get there, click on the **WinMosaic Viewers** link on the *Mosaic Handbook Hotlist* page. The *External Viewer Information* document is shown in Figure 4-19. When you click on a link to a viewer, for instance, LView, the **Save As** dialog box opens and asks you to specify a filename and location for the file. Mosaic then

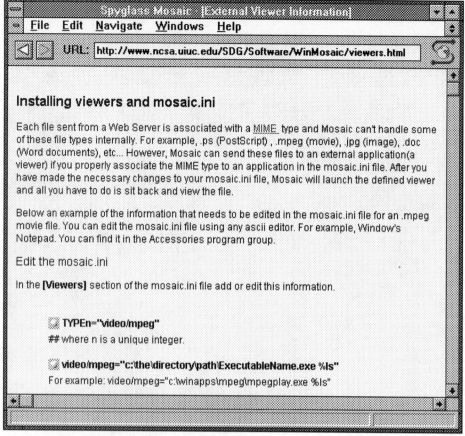

Figure 4–19. WinMosaic External Viewer Information page

downloads the file to your PC. At least it seems that the process is that simple. Here's what actually happens when you click on the link:

1. Mosaic connects to **ftp.ncsa.uiuc.edu**.

2. Mosaic logs you in as an anonymous user.

3. Mosaic sends an FTP request to transfer the file in binary mode.

4. The server downloads the requested file to your computer.

5. Mosaic closes the connection.

Network News

If you have correctly set up your news server in the EMOSAIC.INI file (see Chapter 5, *Customizing Mosaic*, for details), you will be able to use Mosaic as a news-reader. It's not a very full-featured newsreader, but if you don't use network news intensively, you may be happy reading news through Mosaic. If not, consider getting one of the dedicated newsreaders for the PC, such as AIR News, found in the Internet In A Box product from O'Reilly & Associates and Spry, Inc.

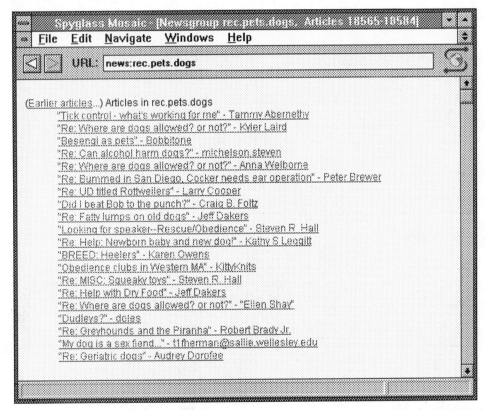

Figure 4–20. Messages in rec.pets.dogs

To get started, simply enter the URL for the newsgroup in the **Open URL** dialog. The syntax is:

```
news:newsgroup-name
```

Mosaic does not allow you to specify different news hosts. You define your news server in your .INI file, and so the URL for news does not have a hostname.

To read postings to *rec.pets.dogs*, the URL is *news:rec.pets.dogs*. Mosaic will connect to your news server and display the most recent messages, as shown in

Figure 4-20. At the top of the screen is a link that reads **Earlier articles**. Clicking on this link displays the next most recent messages. Clicking on a message subject displays that message, as shown in Figure 4-21.

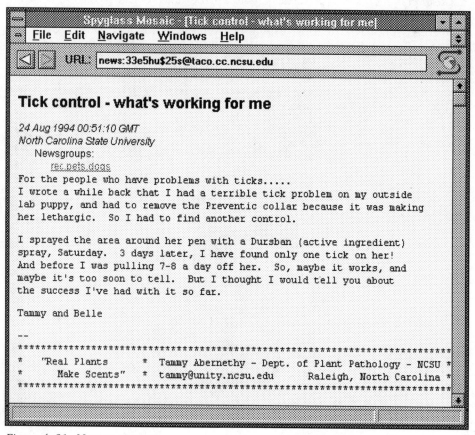

Figure 4–21. Message contents

The message body contains links to earlier and later messages in the thread. Clicking on these will, of course, display the linked message.

Unfortunately, after reading a message, there's not much you can do except send personal email to the author. Mosaic doesn't let you respond to messages or post new articles. In fact, there are a number of other drawbacks to using Mosaic as a newsreader:

- You can't use Mosaic to browse a list of all available newsgroups. You have to know the name of the group you want to read.

- You can only access one group at a time.

- You have to enter the URL for the newsgroup or save it in your hotlist.

- While you can save messages as text files, you can't download graphics or sound files, which are included in some newsgroups, such as *alt.binaries.multimedia* and *alt.pictures.find-art.graphics.*

As Mosaic continues to develop, we expect that it will improve as a client for Gopher, WAIS, FTP, news, and perhaps even email.

CHAPTER FIVE

CUSTOMIZING MOSAIC

Changing Your Home Page
Changing Preferences
Advanced Customization
The Format of EMOSAIC.INI

Mosaic is a powerful tool that allows you to explore information and the connections between information in a multimedia environment. But, as we'll see in this chapter, Mosaic is also a flexible environment that can be customized and extended in many different ways. The combination is what makes Mosaic such an exciting tool: Mosaic not only lets you view information, but also gives you control over how the information will be presented.

The most obvious aspect that you can control is type formatting. As a Windows client, Mosaic can take advantage of the fonts loaded on your system to format many different elements of text in many different ways and to combine them within a document. But you can customize several other parts of the interface as well.

In the current version of Enhanced NCSA Mosaic, only a few customization options are accessible through the **Preferences** dialog box. Future versions will include more customization options, but for now, advanced configuration options are only available by editing Mosaic's initialization file, EMOSAIC.INI.

Granted, this is a lot less pleasant than choosing items from a dialog box, but if you are willing to dive into the configuration file, you will have much more control over Mosaic. EMOSAIC.INI lets you configure four major areas of the program: functionality, display settings, style sheets, and performance. Before we discuss these areas, however, we'll discuss changing your home page and setting the options in the **Preferences** dialog box.

Changing Your Home Page

The home page is a wonderful navigational device that does double duty as map and safe port. Your home page—the document Mosaic retrieves and displays when you launch the program—serves first as your personal navigational map of the Web.

When you're roaming the Net, freely following links and sailing from one server to another, it is not uncommon to find yourself someplace you don't particularly want to be and with no apparent means of getting back out again. When this happens, your home page is your safe haven, a return to your familiar map. Whenever you get to a point where you'd like to start fresh, just return to your home page.

The Home Page that comes with this book has links to *GNN* and the *Mosaic Handbook Hotlist.* While this is an excellent starting point, after you've used Mosaic for a while, you may want to change your home page.

There are a number of reasons you may want to specify a different document as your home page. If you use, say, the *GNN Personal Finance* Center frequently, you may want to use the *Personal Finance Home Page* as your home page. If you have certain areas of specific interest, you may want to have a more narrowly focused home page. For example, if you're particularly interested in astronomy and space, you may want to select "NASA Information Services Via the WWW" as your home page.

Or if you have discovered a number of servers you return to regularly, you may want to create your own custom map of the Web, which you can keep on your local system and update as needed. You might include URLs to your favorite sports, music, and travel servers, if those are your interests. On the other hand, you might prefer to use your hotlist to navigate to your favorite servers and keep a remote server as your home page.

Using Another Document as Your Home Page

To change your home page, simply enter the URL of the new home page in the **Home Page** field of the **Preferences** dialog. But how do you find the URL? The best way is to go there—using your hotlist if you have saved it there; using **History** or hypertext links if you haven't. For instance, if you wanted to use *GNN's The Whole Internet Catalog* as your home page, you would go to the *WIC*, select and copy the URL from the display in the toolbar, and paste it into the field in the **Preferences** dialog.

You can also set your home page in EMOSAIC.INI by changing the Home_Page line. See the "Advanced Customization" section, below, on how to do this.

Creating Your Own Home Page

Creating your own HTML document to use as your home page is a little more involved, but if you want to use your hotlist as your home page, Mosaic's **Export** command (found in the **Hotlist** and **History** dialogs) makes it a snap. **Export** creates an HTML page consisting of all the documents in your hotlist. Every document title is a hypertext link to the actual page on the Net. Here's how to use **Export** to create your own home page:

1. Choose **Hotlist** from the **Navigate** menu.

2. Add and delete items from your hotlist as desired.

3. Click on the **Export** button to export the hotlist to an HTML page.

4. Save this document as a file on your hard disk with the extension .HTM, for example, HOMEPG.HTM. Mosaic then automatically displays this page. Figure 5-1 gives an example.

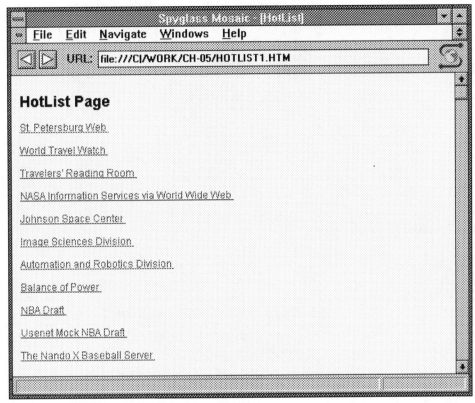

Figure 5–1. Exported hotlist file viewed in Mosaic

5. If you want to rearrange the list or add subject headers, open your home page file in a text editor. The file is coded in HTML and will look something like this:

```
<title>HotList</title>
<h1>HotList Page<\h1>
<a href="http://www.spb.su/">
St. Petersburg Web
</a>
<a href="http://gnn.com/meta/travel/travelwatch2.html">
World Travel Watch
</a>
<a href="http://gnn.com/meta/travel/readingroom.html">
Travelers' Reading Room
```

```
</a>
<a href="http://hypatia.gsfc.nasa.gov/NASA_homepage.html">
NASA Information Services via World Wide Web
</a>
<a href="http://sd-www.jsc.nasa.gov/jscover.html">
Johnson Space Center
</a>
<a href="http://images.jsc.nasa.gov/html/home.htm">
Image Sciences Division
</a>
<a href="http://tommy.jsc.nasa.gov/">
Automation and Robotics Division
</a>
<a href="http://gnn.com/news/sports/strike/strike-intro.html">
Balance of Power
</a>
<a href="http://gnn.com/news/sports/draft/draft-94.html">
NBA Draft
</a>
<a href="http://gnn.com/news/sports/draft/index.html">
Usenet Mock NBA Draft
</a>
<a href="http://www.nando.net/baseball/bbserv.html">
The Nando X Baseball Server
</a>
```

6. Ignoring the coding for now, you should be able to see that each paragraph is the URL and name of a document in the hotlist. Using the cut and paste functions, you can rearrange the paragraphs to group documents by subject or by title. In this case, we might group the documents into *Sports*, *Travel*, and *Space*.

7. You can try a simple bit of tagging to change the title and main heading and add subject headings to the list:

   - Change the title by changing the first line to:

   ```
   <title>My Home Page</title>
   ```

   - Change the main heading by changing the second line to:

   ```
   <h1>My Home Page</h1>
   ```

   - Insert subject headings by adding new paragraphs using this form:

   ```
   <h2>Sports</h2>
   ```

   - Your edited file will look something like this:

   ```
   <title>My Home Page</title>
   <h1>My Home Page</h1>
   <h2>Travel</h2>
   <a href="http://www.spb.su/">
   St. Petersburg Web
   </a>
   <a href="http://gnn.com/meta/travel/travelwatch2.html">
   ```

```
World Travel Watch
</a>
<a href="http://gnn.com/meta/travel/readingroom.html">
Travelers' Reading Room
</a>
<h2>Space</h2>
<a href="http://hypatia.gsfc.nasa.gov/NASA_homepage.html">
NASA Information Services via World Wide Web
</a>
<a href="http://sd-www.jsc.nasa.gov/jscover.html">
Johnson Space Center
</a>
<a href="http://images.jsc.nasa.gov/html/home.htm">
Image Sciences Division
</a>
<a href="http://tommy.jsc.nasa.gov/">
Automation and Robotics Division
</a>
<h2>Sports</h2>
<a href="http://gnn.com/news/sports/strike/strike-intro.html">
Balance of Power
</a>
<a href="http://gnn.com/news/sports/draft/draft-94.html">
NBA Draft
</a>
<a href="http://gnn.com/news/sports/draft/index.html">
Usenet Mock NBA Draft
</a>
<a href="http://www.nando.net/baseball/bbserv.html">
The Nando X Baseball Server
</a>
```

8. After you save your file, you can preview the results by using Mosaic's **Open Local** command and selecting the file. Figure 5-2 shows what our example file looks like in Mosaic.

9. Finally, type in the URL of your new home page file, either in the **Home Page** field of the **Preferences** dialog or in the Home_Page line of the EMOSAIC.INI file. For local files, the URL consists of *File:///*, followed by the pathname. For example, the URL for your original home page is:

```
File:///C:\WIN32APP\EMOSAIC\HOMEPAGE.HTM
```

Once you get into composing HTML, you can do quite a bit more with your home page, including adding graphics, writing lists, and incorporating multiple levels of headings. For instructions on writing HTML and a discussion of creating your own home page, see Chapter 7, *Creating HTML Documents*.

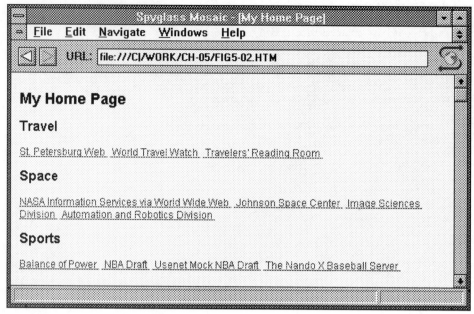

Figure 5–2. Edited home page file

Changing Preferences

The basic configuration options available in **Preferences** allow you to change style sheets, set your home page, and specify whether images will be downloaded automatically.

The options available in **Preferences** are:

- Load Images Automatically
- Underline Links
- Set Home Page
- Proxy Server
- Style Sheets

Load Images Automatically

If you connect to the Internet by dialing in over a SLIP or PPP connection, even with a fast modem, Mosaic may run slower than you would like. The bottleneck is in downloading graphics, especially large ones. By unchecking the **Load Images Automatically** checkbox, you can tell Mosaic not to automatically download images. Instead, Mosaic will draw generic picture icons, as shown in Figure 5-3.

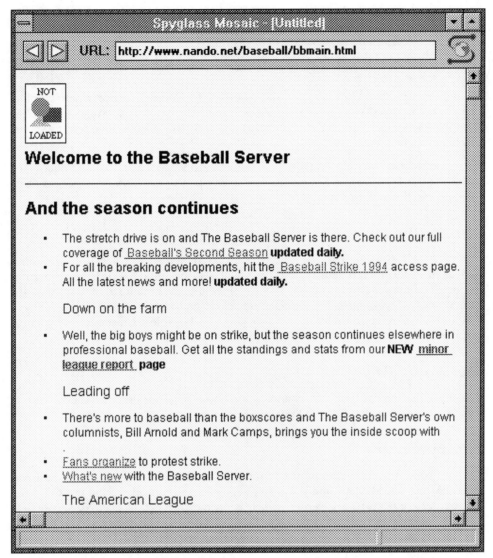

Figure 5-3. Generic picture icons, displayed when Load Images Automatically is off

This speeds things up considerably but, as you can see from the example, really detracts from the design of the page. (If you're working from an office with a dedicated line, you won't need to worry too much about speed.)

Since a lot of the enjoyment of using Mosaic comes from looking at the images on Web pages, you'll want to avoid turning images off. Still, there may be some graphics-laden pages that you use mostly for navigation purposes. Since you know what these pages look like, you can save quite a bit of time by turning images off.

If you do turn images off, you can get the graphics by choosing **Load Missing Images** from the **Navigate** menu to load all the images on a page. Although it's more time consuming to download images this way, using this option gets you the text of the page fairly quickly, so you can decide if you're even interested in the images.

Some servers, like *GNN*, specify alternate text for Mosaic to use when graphics can't be displayed. In these cases, Mosaic will display the alternate text. If the graphics serve as hypertext, the alternate text will have a bounding box, as shown in Figure 5-4.

To reset Mosaic so that images load automatically, go back to **Preferences** and click on the **Load Images Automatically** checkbox. The next time you connect to a server, you'll get all the images.

Underline Links

If you have a color monitor, Mosaic will display hypertext in color. If this option is checked in the **Preferences** dialog, links will also be underlined. Unchecking this option will improve performance slightly, since it takes additional time to draw the underlines. If you have a black-and-white or grayscale monitor, however, you should leave **Anchor Underline** on, so you will be able to distinguish hypertext from regular text.

Set Home Page

As described above, you can change your home page by entering a new URL in the **Set Home Page** field of the **Preferences** window.

Proxy Server

If you work at a site with a security firewall, you won't be able to access the Internet directly. The workaround is a proxy server located outside of the firewall. Your computer connects to this server, which is on the Internet. The **Proxy Server** field in the **Preferences** dialog lets you specify the address of this proxy server. If you're in this situation, ask your network administrator for help.

Style Sheets

Mosaic lets you control how documents will look by choosing a style sheet. Most word processing and page layout programs use "styles," which let you tag a paragraph of text with certain attributes. For instance, in Microsoft Word for Windows, you can select a paragraph of text, set up a style for it (for example, *heading 1*), and then define that style as, say, Times Roman, 36 points, single-spaced, no indent. In other words, you explicitly tell Word the values of the style and the program applies those values whenever you tag a paragraph with that style.

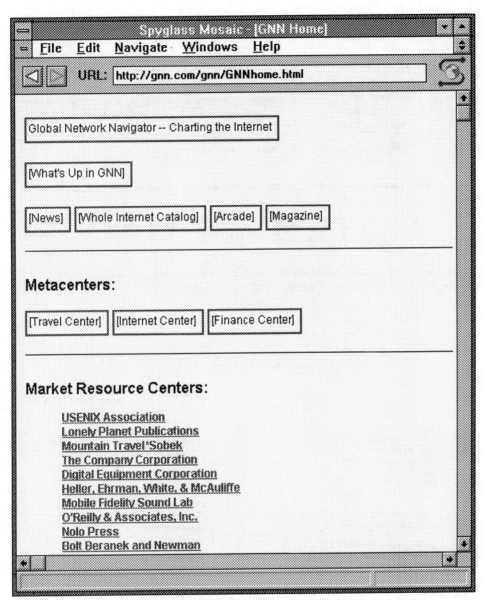

Figure 5–4. Alternate text, displayed when available

HTML operates very differently. There's nothing in an HTML document that specifies font or point size or spacing. All of these style issues are handled by Mosaic. All HTML says is: "This paragraph is heading 1." Mosaic then looks up the settings for the *heading 1* tag and displays the paragraph that way on your computer.

Since you can edit these settings, you can change the way Mosaic displays documents on your screen. Mosaic makes the process even easier by providing global style sheets. Each style sheet has values for every HTML tag, and you can change the overall look of a document just by changing to a different style sheet. Here's how it works:

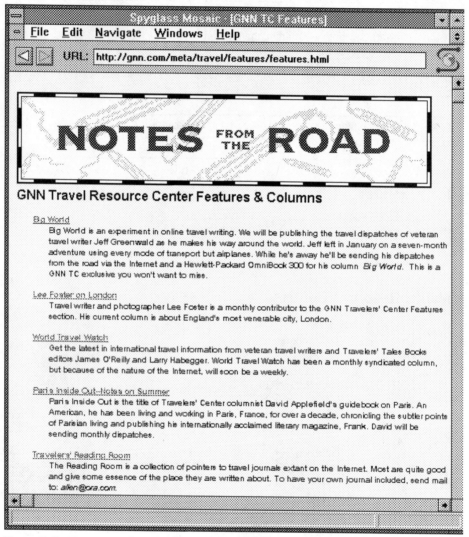

Figure 5–5. Notes From the Road formatted with Sans Serif Small style sheet

1. As an example, go to "Notes From the Road" in the *Travelers' Center*. Figure 5-5 shows this page formatted with the Sans Serif Small style sheet.

2. Then choose **Preferences** from the **Edit** menu and click on the **Style Sheets** pop-up menu. This lets you choose a different style sheet from a list of available choices. Choose **Mixed Large**.

3. Mosaic immediately updates the display using the new style sheet, as shown in Figure 5-6.

Figure 5–6. Notes From the Road formatted with Mixed Large style sheet

If you want to fine-tune any of the style sheets, or if you want to make one from scratch, you need to edit Mosaic's configuration file. We'll show you how to do that in the Advanced Customization section, below.

Advanced Customization

Once you have your home page all set up, you can begin thinking about the other modifications you'd like to make, such as changing the color of hypertext links and setting up new style sheets. To make these and most other customizations, you have to edit the EMOSAIC.INI file.

When Mosaic is launched, it first checks EMOSAIC.INI to find out how it should treat a whole range of attributes that control the way the program functions and how it displays elements on your screen.

A few caveats are in order before you dive in. First, modifying EMOSAIC.INI can have unexpected consequences, one of which is that, in some rare circumstances, Mosaic may not function correctly or may even crash. Therefore, when modifying EMOSAIC.INI, be sure to make and save a copy of your original initialization file. This way you can always go back to an earlier initialization file that was more or less bug-free.

NOTE

Windows 3.x initialization files can be read and modified by any text editor, like Notepad or Word for Windows; however, you may find it easier with a specialized editing utility. A good one is INIEdit, available from Charles E. Kindel, Jr., 22925 N.E. 12th Place, Redmond, WA 98053.

As you make changes to your working copy of EMOSAIC.INI, it is also helpful to include "internal documentation" that makes it clear where you've made changes and what the original values of individual keywords were. You can do this by starting a new line with the word "Rem" or with a semicolon. When Mosaic encounters lines that start with either Rem or a semicolon, it ignores the rest of the line. A couple of lines of a sample file show how this might look:

```
Display_Inline_Images=no
; Changed this from yes
```

As a general rule, you should quit Mosaic before editing the EMOSAIC.INI file. In the first place, most changes won't take effect until you restart the program. This is because most of the settings contained within the initialization file are read only once, when Mosaic is loaded, and are stored in memory thereafter. But more importantly, it is possible that Mosaic may overwrite the new values with its previous values, and all your hard work will be for naught.

The Format of EMOSAIC.INI

Initialization files in Windows are simple lists in which keywords that describe application behavior are defined with certain values. The syntax is:

```
keyword=value
```

Some keywords take a yes or no answer (or true or false, if you prefer; either is acceptable, although it's best to be consistent); other keywords need a specific file or font name. Still others need values in a specific format. In the discussion below, we include tables that show possible values and default settings for each attribute.

For the sake of readability, EMOSAIC.INI is organized into sections, with the section name appearing in brackets. While you should keep the keywords within their indicated sections, the sections can be in any order. The following example shows an EMOSAIC.INI file that includes all the attributes that Mosaic understands. This is not the actual initialization file that is included on your disk.

```
[Main]
Display_Inline_Images=yes
Anchor_Underline=yes
Help_File=help/mo-
help.htm
Hotlist_File=hotlist.htm
Grey Background=no
Anchor_Visitation_Horizon=1

[Styles]
Default_Style_Sheet=Normal
Count_Style_Sheets=2
StyleSheet_Name_1=Normal
Normal_Normal_font=Times New Roman, NoBold, 12, NoItalic, NoUnderline
Normal_H1_font=Times New Roman, Bold, 18, NoItalic, NoUnderline
Normal_H2_font=Times New Roman, Bold, 16, NoItalic, NoUnderline
Normal_H3_font=Times New Roman, NoBold, 16, NoItalic, NoUnderline
Normal_H4_font=Times New Roman, Bold, 14, NoItalic, NoUnderline
Normal_H5_font=Times New Roman, NoBold, 14, NoItalic, NoUnderline
Normal_H6_font=Times New Roman, Bold, 14, NoItalic, NoUnderline
Normal_Listing_Font=Courier New, NoBold, 12, NoItalic, NoUnderline
Normal_Pre_font=Courier New, NoBold, 10, NoItalic, NoUnderline
Normal_Address_font=Times New Roman, NoBold, 12, NoItalic, NoUnderline
Normal_BlockQuote_font=Times New Roman, NoBold, 12, NoItalic, NoUnderline
StyleSheet_Name_2=Medium
Medium_Normal_font=Times New Roman, NoBold, 14, NoItalic, NoUnderline
Medium_H1_font=Times New Roman, Bold, 36, NoItalic, NoUnderline
Medium_H2_font=Times New Roman, Bold, 30, NoItalic, NoUnderline
Medium_H3_font=Times New Roman, NoBold, 24, NoItalic, NoUnderline
Medium_H4_font=Times New Roman, Bold, 18, NoItalic, NoUnderline
Medium_H5_font=Times New Roman, NoBold, 18, NoItalic, NoUnderline
Medium_H6_font=Times New Roman, Bold, 18, NoItalic, NoUnderline
Medium_Listing_Font=Courier New, NoBold, 14, NoItalic, NoUnderline
Medium_Pre_font=Courier New, NoBold, 12, NoItalic, NoUnderline
```

```
Medium_Address_font=Times New Roman, NoBold, 12, NoItalic, NoUnderline
Medium_BlockQuote_font=Times New Roman, NoBold, 12, NoItalic, NoUnderline

[Viewers]
TYPE0=application/postscript
application/postscript=c:\gs\gsnt.exe %s

[Suffixes]
application/postscript=.ps

[Services]
NNTP_Server=
Proxy_Server=

[Settings]
Anchor_Color=0, 0, 255
Anchor_Color_Visited=255, 0, 0

[Document Caching]
Number=4

[Image Caching]
Number=50

[Main Window]
width=500
height=400

[PageSetup]
margin_left=0.75
margin_right=0.75
margin_top=0.75
margin_bottom=0.75
```

In this chapter, we have chosen not to follow the sections of the EMOSAIC.INI file, since that organization is neither particularly useful nor required. Instead we have chosen to organize the attributes into four major groups:

- Functional attributes

- Display attributes

- Style sheets

- Performance

Functional Attributes

By editing certain lines in EMOSAIC.INI you can control functions such as the downloading of images and the use of external programs to display certain files. Table 5-1 shows a chart of the functional attributes.

Table 5-1: Functional Attributes in EMOSAIC.INI

Attribute	Possible Values	Default or Example
[Main]		
Display_Inline_Images	yes/no	yes
Help_File	filename	help/mo-help.htm
Hotlist_File	filename	hotlist.htm
Home_Page	filename or URL	http:/gnn.com/GNNhome.html
[Viewers]		
TYPEn	MIME type/subtype	application/postscript
MIME type/subtype	command line	c:/gs/gsnt.exe
[Suffixes]		
MIME type/subtype	file extension	.ps
[Encodings]		
MIME type/subtype	encoding setting	8bit
[Services]		
NNTP_Server	server name	news.ora.com
Proxy_Server	server name	proxy.ora.com

Display_Inline_Images

This attribute has the same function as the **Load Images Automatically** option in the **Preferences** dialog. It determines whether inline images (the images that are part of a page) will be automatically displayed with the document. (See the "Performance" section later in this chapter for a discussion of when you might want to disable this function.) Since it's easier to control this setting through the dialog box, leave this key set to **yes**.

Hotlist_File

This keyword specifies the file that Mosaic uses to store your hotlist. The default is HOTLIST.HTM. The hotlist file is a standard HTML document with the URLs of the documents you saved in your hotlist. So, if you have another hotlist file that you want to use instead, you can set Mosaic to use that document instead by changing HOTLIST.HTM to the name of your file.

Home_Page

As discussed above, home pages can be specified in either the **Preferences** dialog or with this attribute in EMOSAIC.INI. While individual users will have more flexibility by setting the home page in **Preferences**, system administrators might want to use the .INI file in order to give a group of users a standard home page. When you first open EMOSAIC.INI, this line will look something like this:

```
Home_Page=File:\\\WIN32APP\EMOSAIC\HOMEPAGE.HTML
```

To change the default home page, change the URL to that of the new home page.

Viewers

Several of the sections of EMOSAIC.INI allow you to configure other programs, called external viewers, which Mosaic launches as needed to display files that it can't handle internally. For instance, Mosaic cannot display video files in the MPEG format. Instead, it launches an MPEG player program, which runs the file in a separate window. Mosaic lets you specify which programs to use with which file formats. In this way, Mosaic is an extensible multimedia viewer; as new media formats become available, you can simply configure Mosaic to use appropriate viewers. (The use of external viewers will be discussed at length in Chapter 6, *Using Mosaic for Multimedia*.)

Enhanced NCSA Mosaic doesn't come with any external viewers; you have to download them yourself from various sites on the Internet. (We'll tell how and where in Chapter 6.) Once you've obtained the programs, you have to tell Mosaic how to use them by editing the Viewers section of EMOSAIC.INI.

Mosaic uses the *Multipurpose Internet Mail Extensions* (*MIME*) protocol to deal with these external viewers. MIME defines a number of content types and subtypes, which allow MIME-capable programs like Mosaic to recognize different kinds of files and deal with them appropriately.

The MIME type specifies the format of the file—such as image, audio, or video—and the subtype gives the precise file format. Under the type *image* there are various subtypes, including *jpeg, gif,* and *tiff.* MIME types are specified by number using the form TYPE*n*. Any number of MIME types can be specified, but the numbering must be in order, starting with TYPE0, TYPE1, and so on.

So, in the Viewers section, there are two steps to defining viewers: first, match a type number to a MIME type/subtype; second, tell Mosaic what application to use when it encounters a file of that type. The following example sets the definition for viewing MPEG movies:

```
[Viewers]
TYPE0=video/mpeg
video/mpeg=c:\WIN32APP\EMOSAIC\MPEG\MPEGPLAY.EXE %S
```

In this example, the first line defines TYPE0 as MPEG video files, and the second line tells Mosaic the command line to use to launch MPEGPlay, a program that plays MPEG movies. The characters %S at the end of the command line tell the viewer to display the downloaded file.

Although it is not required, you can provide Mosaic with the extensions of files of a certain type. For instance, you can inform Mosaic that video/mpeg files have an extension of *.mpg*. To do this, add the following lines to EMOSAIC.INI:

```
[Suffixes]
video/mpeg=.mpeg, .mp, .mpg
```

Table 5-2 gives examples of some of the MIME types, appropriate Windows programs, and some possible file suffixes. The exact command line you use in your

EMOSAIC.INI file depends on where you install these programs. See Chapter 6 for more detail about installing and using these programs.

Table 5–2: MIME Types, Associated External Viewers, and Possible Suffixes

MIME Type	Program	Suffixes
image/gif	LView	.gif
image/jpeg	LView	.jpeg, .jpg
video/mpeg	MPEGPlay	.mpeg, .mpg
video/quicktime	Quick Time Video Player	.qt, .moov, .moo
application/postscript	GhostScript	.ps, .eps

Services

To use network news or a proxy server through Mosaic, you need to set the appropriate server names in the Services section of EMOSAIC.INI. (The proxy server can also be set in the **Preferences** dialog box.)

NNTP_Server

This is the news server that Mosaic connects to when you contact a network news group, such as *rec.music.folk*. Your workplace or Internet provider probably runs a network news server. That's the server name you should use for this attribute, for example:

```
NNTP_Server=news.ora.com
```

If you don't specify a news server in EMOSAIC.INI, you won't be able to read network news via Mosaic.

Proxy_Server

A proxy server lets people behind a security firewall gain access to the Internet without compromising security. Proxy servers are also used to increase performance by holding lots of documents in a cache and then quickly passing them on to users as requested. In these cases, your system administrator may want to set the proxy server in the EMOSAIC.INI file. At O'Reilly & Associates, we might set this attribute to:

```
Proxy_Server=proxy.ora.com
```

Display Attributes

The display attributes control the way Mosaic presents information, sizes windows, displays pages, and so on. Table 5-3 shows the display attributes, possible values, and default settings.

Table 5-3: Display Attributes in EMOSAIC.INI

Attribute	Possible Values	Default or Example
[Settings]		
Anchor_Color	RGB values	0, 0. 255
Anchor_Color_Visited	RGB values	255, 0, 0
[Main]		
Anchor_Underline	yes/no	yes
Anchor_Visitation_Horizon	number	1
Grey Background	yes/no	no
[Main Window]		
Width	n pixels	500
Height	n pixels	400
[PageSetup]		
Margin_Left	n inches	0.75
Margin_Right	n inches	0.75
Margin_Top	n inches	0.75
Margin_Bottom	n inches	0.75

Hypertext colors

When running on a color system, Mosaic is set to display hypertext anchors in blue and visited hypertext anchors (the ones you've been to) in red. You can change these settings using the `Anchor_Color` and `Anchor_Color_Visited` attributes. Here are the default settings in EMOSAIC.INI:

```
[Settings]
Anchor_Color=0, 0, 255
Anchor_Color_Visited=255, 0, 0
```

To understand these settings, a little color theory is perhaps in order. Computer monitors display color by shooting combinations of red, green, and blue light at your screen. Each of the three light sources can be set for one of 256 levels of intensity, from 0 to 255, with 0 being all the way off and 255 being all the way on. So, the three numbers in these keywords specify a color in terms of red, green, and blue, or RGB, color.

The `Anchor_Color` attribute sets the color of hypertext. With these settings, Mosaic displays hypertext in blue. That's because red (the first number) is set to 0, green (the second number) is set to 0, and blue (the third number) is set to 255.

Likewise, the visited anchor key, which sets the color of hypertext after you've visited the linked document, is set to red because red is all the way on and green and blue are off.

You can change these settings to any colors you want. Table 5-4 shows the RGB values for some basic colors. To discover the RGB values for other colors, try working in a program that provides a color-mixing palette, write down the RGB values for the colors you like, and then enter them in this section of EMOSAIC.INI.

Table 5–4: Some Common Colors and Their RGB Values

Color	Red	Green	Blue
Black	0	0	0
Dark Green	0	128	0
Light Blue	0	255	255
Olive	128	128	0
Dark Grey	128	128	128
Light Grey	192	192	192
Magenta	255	0	128
Purple	255	0	255
Yellow	255	255	0
White	255	255	255

Anchor_Visitation_Horizon

If you haven't visited a document in a certain amount of time, it seems reasonable to consider that link unvisited. Mosaic lets you set that time period with the Anchor_Visitation_Horizon attribute. This specifies the number of days before a visited anchor reverts to a normal anchor. When set to 1, visited anchors are only in effect for a day. When set to 2, two days, and so on. When the attribute is set to 0, Mosaic does not change the display of links; visited links are not distinguished from unvisited links.

Anchor Underline

This line is automatically created by Mosaic when you change the underline setting in the **Preferences** dialog. The default is for underlining to be on.

Grey Background

Do you prefer reading documents against a white or grey background? Mosaic is set to use a white background (Grey Background=no) but many people creating documents assume you have a grey background, so you might want to change this setting to **yes**.

Window Setup

The Document Windows section controls the size of new document windows in Mosaic. If not specified, new document windows are the same size as the main window. To change the size of new windows, enter a Document Windows section in EMOSAIC.INI, specifying the width and height in pixels.

```
[Document Window]
width=500
height=400
```

If you have a large monitor, you may wish to change these settings. Simply change the numbers in the values for width and height.

Page Setup

You can change the way documents are displayed within Mosaic's window by editing this section of EMOSAIC.INI. The values for the margin settings are in inches. Here are the default settings:

```
[PageSetup]
margin_left=0.75
margin_right=0.75
margin_top=0.75
margin_bottom=0.75
```

Style Sheets

As we discussed above, you can change the appearance of documents by changing the style sheet in the **Preferences** menu. But what if you don't like Mosaic's standard style sheets? What if you want to use some of the fonts on your system and mix them in wild and wooly ways? Your graphic designer friends might bristle, but they're your fonts to use or abuse as you wish.

By editing the Styles section of EMOSAIC.INI, you can change the settings for existing style sheets or create brand new ones. Then you can change the way Mosaic displays text by selecting a different style sheet in the **Preferences** dialog box. The display will update immediately. Table 5-5 shows the attributes of the Styles section.

Table 5-5: Attributes and Values for the Styles Section of EMOSAIC.INI

Attribute	Possible Value	Default
Default_Style_Sheet	Style sheet name	Normal
Count_Style_Sheets	Number of style sheets	2
Style_Sheet_Name_n	Style sheet name	Normal
StyleSheetName_HTML	Font, bold status,	Normal_H1_font=Times
Tag_font	point size, italic status,	New Roman, NoBold, 12,
	underline status	NoItalic, NoUnderline

To get started, let's take a look at a sample Styles section in EMOSAIC.INI:

```
[Styles]
Default_Style_Sheet=Normal
Count_Style_Sheets=2
StyleSheet_Name_1=Normal
```

```
Normal_Normal_font=Times New Roman, NoBold, 12, NoItalic, NoUnderline
Normal_H1_font=Times New Roman, Bold, 18, NoItalic, NoUnderline
Normal_H2_font=Times New Roman, Bold, 16, NoItalic, NoUnderline
Normal_H3_font=Times New Roman, NoBold, 16, NoItalic, NoUnderline
Normal_H4_font=Times New Roman, Bold, 14, NoItalic, NoUnderline
Normal_H5_font=Times New Roman, NoBold, 14, NoItalic, NoUnderline
Normal_H6_font=Times New Roman, Bold, 14, NoItalic, NoUnderline
Normal_Listing_Font=Courier New, NoBold, 12, NoItalic, NoUnderline
Normal_Pre_font=Courier New, NoBold, 10, NoItalic, NoUnderline
Normal_Address_font=Times New Roman, NoBold, 12, NoItalic, NoUnderline
Normal_BlockQuote_font=Times New Roman, NoBold, 12, NoItalic, NoUnderline
StyleSheet_Name_2=Medium
Medium_Normal_font=Times New Roman, NoBold, 14, NoItalic, NoUnderline
Medium_H1_font=Times New Roman, Bold, 36, NoItalic, NoUnderline
Medium_H2_font=Times New Roman, Bold, 30, NoItalic, NoUnderline
Medium_H3_font=Times New Roman, NoBold, 24, NoItalic, NoUnderline
Medium_H4_font=Times New Roman, Bold, 18, NoItalic, NoUnderline
Medium_H5_font=Times New Roman, NoBold, 18, NoItalic, NoUnderline
Medium_H6_font=Times New Roman, Bold, 18, NoItalic, NoUnderline
Medium_Listing_Font=Courier New, NoBold, 14, NoItalic, NoUnderline
Medium_Pre_font=Courier New, NoBold, 12, NoItalic, NoUnderline
Medium_Address_font=Times New Roman, NoBold, 12, NoItalic, NoUnderline
Medium_BlockQuote_font=Times New Roman, NoBold, 12, NoItalic, NoUnderline
```

There are two style sheets in this example: Normal and Medium. The Medium style sheet generally uses bigger and bolder fonts than the Normal style sheet. Most of the attributes in this section refer to the tags in HTML documents, which tell Mosaic how to format the document. While we won't explain all the tags here (see Chapter 7 for an in-depth treatment of HTML), we'll go through a few to give you an idea of how to edit style sheets.

Default_Style_Sheet

This attribute specifies which style sheet Mosaic will use when it starts up. The default is set to Normal but you can change it to the name of any style sheet that you set up.

Count_Style_Sheets

This attribute tells Mosaic how many style sheets are defined. If you add additional style sheets, as explained below, be sure to change the number here to reflect the actual number of style sheets.

Style_Sheet_Name

This attribute defines the name for each style sheet. Notice that the keyword requires the number of the style sheet, while the value is the name of the style sheet. Style sheets must be numbered in order. Thus the keyword for the first style sheet is StyleSheet_Name_1 and the keyword for the second one is StyleSheet_Name_2.

Tag-specific attributes

All the other attributes in a style sheet specify the font to be used with different HTML tags. These tags describe the display elements of a document. (See Appendix B, *HTML Reference Guide* for a complete list of HTML tags.) All of the formatting you see on a Web page is a result of these tags. The first tag in the style sheet is called Normal and is applied to standard text. The first word in the key-word is the name of the style sheet (Normal, in this case) and the second is the name of the HTML tag. So the font for the Normal tag is Times New Roman, no bold, 12 points, no italic, no underline.

There are five font attributes that must be in the value for the tag keys: font name, bold status, point size, italic status, and underline status. You must use all five attributes in exactly that order. Bold, italic, and underline are either on or off. To turn off these formats, the form is NoBold, NoItalic, and NoUnderline.

The syntax is:

```
StyleSheet_Name_number=stylesheet name
Stylesheet Name_Tag_font=Font, (Bold/NoBold), Point Size,
(Italic/NoItalic), (Underline/NoUnderline).
```

The next tag is H1, which is a top-level heading. H2 is a second-level heading, H3 is a third-level heading, and so on, down to H6. Notice that H1 is set for 18-point Times New Roman Bold, H2 is set for 16-point Times New Roman Bold, and H3 is set for 16-point Times New Roman. The lower heading tags all have the same set-tings and are rarely used because they can be difficult to distinguish when displayed.

The other keywords specify fonts for other HTML tags. The most common ones are Listing, which sets the fonts for ordered and unordered lists, Pre, which sets the font for preformatted text, and Address, which sets the font for text in the address format. Again, see Chapter 7 for more information about HTML.

From here, it's a simple matter to change these settings as you wish, using differ-ent fonts, point sizes, and formatting. Here are some points to remember:

- Make sure that the headings are in decreasing order of prominence; that is, an H3 heading should be less prominent (in either point size or formatting) than an H2 heading, and an H2 heading should be less prominent than an H1 head-ing.

- Preformatted text (the Pre tag) must be in a monospaced font like Courier or Monaco.

- Be aware that some fonts are "display" faces and should only be used at large point sizes, while others are "text" faces, which work well as body copy.

If you want to add a new style sheet, there are only a few additional steps.

- If you want your new style sheet to be the default, change the default keyword accordingly.

- Change the number in the count style sheets line to reflect the additional style sheet.

- Rather than writing a new style sheet from scratch, paste a copy of an existing style sheet at the end of the Styles section.

- Change the style sheet name to a new name.

In the following example, we have added a new style sheet called Mixed to the Styles section.

```
[Styles]
Default_Style_Sheet=Mixed
Count_Style_Sheets=3
StyleSheet_Name_1=Normal
Normal_Normal_font=Times New Roman, NoBold, 12, NoItalic, NoUnderline
Normal_H1_font=Times New Roman, Bold, 18, NoItalic, NoUnderline
Normal_H2_font=Times New Roman, Bold, 16, NoItalic, NoUnderline
Normal_H3_font=Times New Roman, NoBold, 16, NoItalic, NoUnderline
Normal_H4_font=Times New Roman, Bold, 14, NoItalic, NoUnderline
Normal_H5_font=Times New Roman, NoBold, 14, NoItalic, NoUnderline
Normal_H6_font=Times New Roman, Bold, 14, NoItalic, NoUnderline
Normal_Listing_Font=Courier New, NoBold, 12, NoItalic, NoUnderline
Normal_Pre_font=Courier New, NoBold, 10, NoItalic, NoUnderline
Normal_Address_font=Times New Roman, NoBold, 12, NoItalic, NoUnderline
Normal_BlockQuote_font=Times New Roman, NoBold, 12, NoItalic, NoUnderline
StyleSheet_Name_1=Normal
Normal_Normal_font=Times New Roman, NoBold, 12, NoItalic, NoUnderline
Normal_H1_font=Times New Roman, Bold, 18, NoItalic, NoUnderline
Normal_H2_font=Times New Roman, Bold, 16, NoItalic, NoUnderline
Normal_H3_font=Times New Roman, NoBold, 16, NoItalic, NoUnderline
Normal_H4_font=Times New Roman, Bold, 14, NoItalic, NoUnderline
Normal_H5_font=Times New Roman, NoBold, 14, NoItalic, NoUnderline
Normal_H6_font=Times New Roman, Bold, 14, NoItalic, NoUnderline
Normal_Listing_Font=Courier New, NoBold, 12, NoItalic, NoUnderline
Normal_Pre_font=Courier New, NoBold, 10, NoItalic, NoUnderline
Normal_Address_font=Times New Roman, NoBold, 12, NoItalic, NoUnderline
Normal_BlockQuote_font=Times New Roman, NoBold, 12, NoItalic, NoUnderline
StyleSheet_Name_3=Mixed
Normal_Normal_font=Palatino, 12, NoItalic, NoUnderline
Normal_H1_font=Helvetica, Bold, 36, NoItalic, NoUnderline
Normal_H2_font=Helvetica, Bold, 30, Italic, NoUnderline
Normal_H3_font=Helvetica, NoBold, 24, Italic, NoUnderline
Normal_H4_font=Helvetica, Bold, 18, NoItalic, NoUnderline
Normal_H5_font=Helvetica, Bold, 18, NoItalic, NoUnderline
Normal_H6_font=Helvetica, Bold, 18, NoItalic, NoUnderline
Normal_Listing_Font=Palatino, NoBold, 12, Italic, NoUnderline
Normal_Pre_font=Courier New, NoBold, 10, NoItalic, NoUnderline
Normal_Address_font=Palatino, NoBold, 12, NoItalic, NoUnderline
Normal_BlockQuote_font=Palatino, NoBold, 12, NoItalic, NoUnderline
```

Notice that the headings are in Helvetica, while the Normal font and most of the other text styles are in Palatino. The Pre tag is set for Courier, which is a monospaced font. We also changed the default to the new style sheet.

Performance

It seems like Mosaic and the Web could always stand to be a little faster, no matter what speed Internet connection you have. The Internet, which spans tens of thousands of miles and connects millions of users, of course bears some of the blame for the delays. And HTTP, the Web protocol, could certainly benefit from some speed enhancements. But there is little individual users can do about either of these factors. So we look to Mosaic to improve performance. There are two main methods for improving Mosaic's performance—caching documents and suppressing the retrieval of inline images. Both are focused on the idea of reducing the amount of time Mosaic spends retrieving documents over the Internet.

Caching

Caches come in a variety of forms, but they all involve some attempt to substitute access to a faster device (like memory) for access to a slower device (like disk drives or remote computers on networks). Without caching, for example, Mosaic must go somewhere in the Internet to retrieve your home page, then go out again to read your next document. If you then decide to return to your home page, it has to go out to retrieve that document all over again.

In a hypermedia system like the World Wide Web, you are likely to return to the same documents over and over again since Mosaic encourages you to follow your trail backward or to return to your home page. But each time that you move backward to a document you've seen previously, Mosaic has to locate it on the network, download it, interpret it, and display it. Clearly, this repetitive searching for and reading of documents over the Internet constitutes a major drain on Mosaic's performance.

To help prevent performance from becoming completely bogged down as it reads and rereads the same documents, Mosaic supports document caching. This means that memory is set aside to hold the contents of documents. When Mosaic reads a document for the first time, it writes the file to memory at the same time it draws it on your screen. The next time, Mosaic simply reads it from the document cache, which is significantly faster than acquiring it over the network.

If document caching is not explicitly controlled within EMOSAIC.INI, Mosaic will cache only the last document that you view. That way, if you switch back from the current document, Mosaic will be able to display that document almost immediately. If you then navigate backward one more document or select a hypertext link to a document that you have not previously viewed, Mosaic will be forced to go out to the Net to find it. As currently configured, however, Mosaic will cache the last four documents that you view.

You can change that number by increasing or decreasing the document caching attribute in EMOSAIC.INI. Similarly, you can change the number of images cached by changing the image caching attribute. The following example shows the default settings.

```
[Document Caching]
Number=4
[Image Caching]
Number=50
```

These settings says that Mosaic can hold four documents and 50 images in the cache. To change the cache setting, just change these numbers. How many documents can Mosaic hold in cache? It depends on how much memory you have. If you set these numbers very high, you will run out of RAM and Mosaic will use virtual memory; however, this will probably still be faster than going out over the network and retrieving them.

Since Mosaic holds so many more images than documents in the cache, reloading a document that is no longer in the cache won't necessarily download the images again. If you want a fresh download of images, you'll have to empty the image cache as well. In this case, use **Open URL** to connect to the server and download the document.

Viewing selected inline images

As we explained above, you can set Mosaic so that it does not automatically display inline images, either by turning off a checkbox in the **Preferences** dialog or by setting Display_Inline_Images to no in the EMOSAIC.INI file. The selection you make in the **Preferences** dialog will override whatever value you set in EMOSAIC.INI. In future versions of the software, you will be able to control many of these settings through menu options rather than by editing the EMOSAIC.INI file.

CHAPTER SIX

USING MOSAIC FOR MULTIMEDIA

What You'll Need
Installing a Viewer
Getting the Big Picture
Digital Drive-In
Sound Waves
Other Viewers and Files

Multimedia on the Internet can be one of the most exciting uses of Mosaic. You can play movies and music, look at full-color images of space or great artwork, run scientific animations and models, display 3D graphics, and more.

But Internet multimedia can sometimes be frustrating and is almost always time-consuming. The problem is that these files can be quite large. For instance, a one-minute MPEG movie can be a megabyte or more, a three-minute song might be four or five megabytes, and large full-color graphics are typically half a megabyte or so.

How long it takes to download a file depends on the kind of network connection you have, how far away the server is, and how busy the network is. If you connect to the Internet over a modem, downloading large files will quietly drive you insane if you sit and stare at Mosaic's progress bar. So, when you start downloading movie and sound files, be prepared to take a break or work in another application.

Even so, using multimedia files on the Net can be worth the pain because the results can be stunning, perhaps even more so because it takes so long to get the files. When you bring up that full-screen version of the Mona Lisa, or sit back and play a four-minute track from an unsigned band, or fly through a computer-generated fractal environment . . . in short, when you sit back, stare at your screen, and say, "Wow!" that's when you'll appreciate the full power of Mosaic.

What You'll Need

While you don't need a Pentium to run Mosaic, the faster your PC, the happier you'll be. Speed becomes even more of an issue when you're working with multi-media files, but processor speed is not the only issue. For instance, how smoothly video plays is affected by processor speed, available memory, and disk speed.

Even with a fast machine and plenty of memory, you won't have much of a multi-media experience if you can't hear sounds or see color. So you'll need a graphics adapter and a monitor capable of displaying at least 256 colors. (If you're buying a new monitor, be sure to get a low-radiation model.) For sound you'll need a sound card and speakers.

The hardware setup is just one part of the puzzle, though; you'll also need soft-ware programs capable of displaying various kinds of files. "Wait a minute," you may be saying, "I have Mosaic. What other software do I need?"

Mosaic cannot directly display all the types of files you might want to use. Instead it relies on other, smaller, programs that are designed to handle specific kinds of files. There are different programs for graphics files, audio files, video files, and so on. When you download a file that Mosaic can't display by itself (basically, any-thing except HTML and text), it launches one of these programs (referred to as "external viewers" because they are external to Mosaic), which then displays the file. These viewers give Mosaic its power as a multimedia application; they make it possible for Mosaic to display the diversity of digital media on the Internet. In this chapter, we'll show you how to view full-color images, watch movies, and listen to sounds. We'll cover finding and downloading viewers, configuring Mosaic to use them properly, and getting and playing files.

Installing a Viewer

There's nothing special about viewer applications; you can use any Windows pro-gram as a viewer for the file types that program handles. Since the main purpose of external viewers is simply to display files, rather than to do a lot of editing, it's best to use small programs that launch quickly and don't require a lot of memory. There are several freeware and shareware programs available on the Internet that make good viewers. There is no central repository for Windows viewers; different programs exist on many different servers. NCSA, however, has tested several pro-grams, which it has verified will work with WinMosaic, NCSA's Windows version of Mosaic. These viewers also work well with Enhanced NCSA Mosaic, the pro-gram that comes with this book. To download some of these programs, go to NCSA's *Windows Viewers* document. You can get there by clicking on the appro-priate link on the *Mosaic Handbook Hotlist* in *GNN*, or enter the URL, using Mosaic's **Open URL** command. The URL is *http://www.ncsa.uiuc.edu/SDG/Software /WinMosaic/viewers.html*.

The document, as shown in Figure 6-1, lists the programs that NCSA has tested and gives brief descriptions of their uses. You can download these programs by clicking on the appropriate hypertext link. In this chapter, we'll download LView (which displays GIF and JPEG graphics files), MPEGPlay (which plays MPEG movies), and WHAM (Waveform Hold and Modify, which plays many different kinds of audio files).

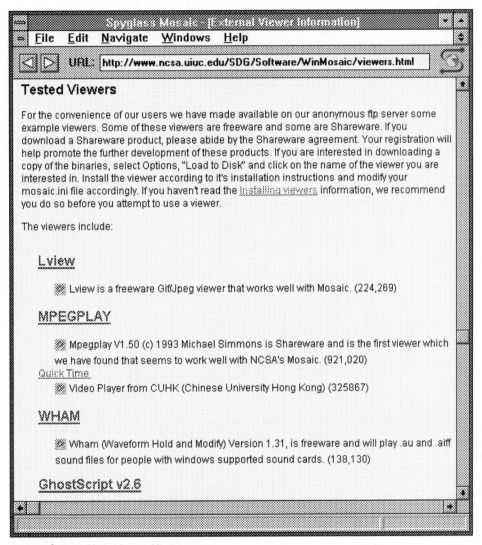

Figure 6-1. NCSA's Mosaic Viewer page

Downloading and Installing LView

Let's start with LView. When you position your cursor over the LView link, Mosaic tells you the URL of the file:

```
ftp://ftp.ncsa.uiuc.edu/PC/Mosaic/Viewers/lview31.zip
```

From this URL you can tell that you'll be using FTP to download the file from NCSA's FTP server. The *.zip* file extension tells you that this is a compressed file. The *.zip* extension is created by the compression program PKZIP, so to decompress it you'll need to use PKUNZIP, a freeware program available from *ftp://beethoven.cs.colostate.edu:/pub/msdos/pk.*

To download and install LView:

1. Using Windows' **File Manager**, make a new directory for LView. You may want to make it a subdirectory within the Spyglass directory.

2. Returning to Mosaic, click on the link for LView. Mosaic will open the **Save As** dialog box. Leave the filename as it is (*lview31.zip*) and select the LView directory. Click on **OK**. Mosaic will then connect you to the FTP server and start the download.

3. When the download is complete, you'll need to decompress the file using PKUNZIP. Unfortunately, this program does not work properly with Windows running, so quit Mosaic and any other Windows applications, and then quit Windows.

4. Now you're ready to decompress *lview31.zip* into the LView directory. Assuming that you created a subdirectory for LView within the Spyglass directory, you would type the following at the DOS prompt:

```
PKUNZIP LVIEW31.ZIP \WIN32APP\EMOSAIC\LVIEW
```

5. PKUNZIP then extracts all the LView files from the compressed file and puts them in the LView directory.

6. Now create a program item for LView, using the **New** command from the Program Manager's **File** menu. See your Windows manual for details of this operation.

Configuring LView

OK, LView is now installed on your machine. The next step is to configure Mosaic to work with LView. This is done by editing the Viewers section of the EMOSAIC.INI file. This is what the relevant part of the .INI file looks like when LView is configured correctly.

```
[Viewers]
TYPE0=image/gif
image/gif=C:\WIN32APP\EMOSAIC\LVIEW/LVIEW31.EXE %s
TYPE1=image/jpeg
image/jpeg=C:\WIN32APP\EMOSAIC\LVIEW/LVIEW31.EXE %s
```

The configuration process basically tells Mosaic which program to run to handle different types of files. There are three parts to the process:

1. Define a type number for each viewer. The first viewer is TYPE0, the next is TYPE1, and so on. Type numbers must be in order, with no missing numbers. That is, you can't jump from TYPE1 to TYPE3.

2. Define a file type for each type number. These file types are actually part of the MIME specification. MIME is a way of telling a program what kind of file it is dealing with. MIME types consist of types and subtypes. For instance, a GIF file is identified as image/gif. Its type is image and its subtype is GIF. A JPEG file is identified as image/jpeg. In both cases, the identifications tell Mosaic what kind of file is to be displayed. The syntax for defining a file type is:

   ```
   type number=file type
   ```

   In the example above, we defined TYPE0 as image/gif, as follows:

   ```
   TYPE0=image/gif
   ```

3. The next step is to tell Mosaic which program to run when GIF files are encountered. The syntax is:

   ```
   file type=application command
   ```

   We want to use LView, of course, so we enter the command line to run LView and open the downloaded file. The line is:

   ```
   image/gif=C:\WIN32APP\EMOSAIC\LVIEW\LVIEW31.EXE %s
   ```

   The command line specifies the location of the program file, then gives the name of the program file (*lview31.exe*). The string %s tells LView to open the downloaded file upon launching. If you're not sure of the name of the program file, look in the directory for a file with an *.exe* extension. That's the program file.

Now, since LView also handles JPEG files, we want to configure Mosaic to launch LView when JPEG files are encountered.

1. Define the next type number, in this case, TYPE1, and match a file type with it, in this case, image/jpeg. So you would type:

   ```
   TYPE1=image/jpeg
   ```

2. Tell Mosaic what command line to use when it encounters JPEG files. Since we're using LView again, the command line is the same:

```
image/jpeg=C:\WIN32APP\EMOSAIC\LVIEW\LVIEW31.EXE %s
```

That's it. Save and close EMOSAIC.INI. Now let's see how Mosaic works together with linked GIF and JPEG files.

Getting the Big Picture

Most of the files on the Web (aside from HTML files, of course) are graphics files. You may be thinking that Mosaic can already display graphics, since *GNN* contains graphics. In fact, as far as the Web is concerned, there are two kinds of graphics. Inline graphics are arranged on HTML pages, while linked graphics are stand-alone graphics files that require an external viewer like LView. There are several graphics formats, although GIF and JPEG are the most common on the Internet.

GIF is an 8-bit indexed color file format, while JPEG is a compression standard for 24-bit color. Quality depends on the level of compression, but JPEG images are generally better quality than GIF images.

After you install LView and configure the EMOSAIC.INI file, you can view some of the great graphics on the Net. To try this, go to the *Space Telescope Science Institute's* page of recent Hubble Space Telescope images.

The URL is *http://marvel.stsci.edu/EPA/Recent.html.*

This page, shown in Figure 6-2, contains thumbnail images of photographs taken by the Hubble Space Telescope. Clicking on the image downloads a larger JPEG version of the image. There's an icon labeled **GIF**, which you can click on to see the GIF version of the image. There's also a caption icon, for seeing a text file about the photograph.

Let's go ahead and get the JPEG version of the Orion Nebula.

1. Click on the thumbnail photos.

2. When the **Save As** dialog box appears, save the file to your hard disk. Make sure you use a *.jpg* extension.

3. When the download is complete, LView will launch and display the file, as shown in Figure 6-3.

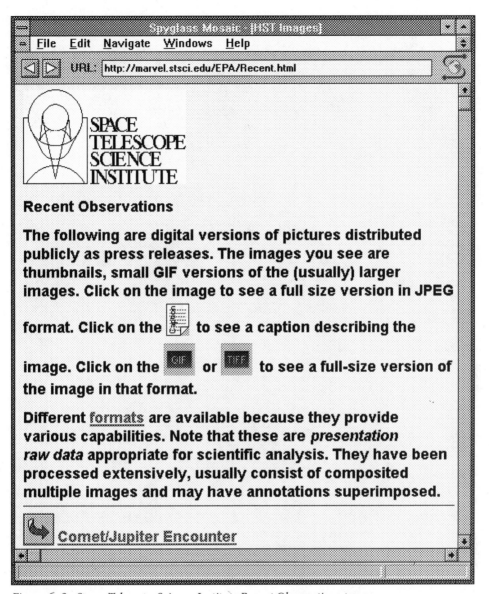

Figure 6-2. Space Telescope Science Institute Recent Observations page

Figure 6–3. Orion Nebula (Photo: C.R. O'Dell (Rice University) and NASA.)

LView is a full-image editing program, so there's a lot you can do with images once you've downloaded them, including changing color, applying special-effects filters, and changing formats.

Digital Drive-In

Playing movies on your computer is one of the cooler ways to waste time at work. Actually, digital video has the potential to be quite useful, as well as fun. Imagine reading an entry from Nixon chief of staff H.R. Haldeman's diaries and being able to view a home movie he took on the day of the journal entry. Or learning a new software program and watching a movie that demonstrates a difficult function. Or reading an author's work and seeing an interview with him.

These are all great uses of video on the network. There aren't many cases where video and text are integrated very tightly, however. Most video clips on the Internet are random clips of a minute or less.

In *Digital Drive-In*, a *GNN* special publication, D.C. Denison explains the state of digital video:

> It's the Internet's final frontier: moving pictures. Every cyberspace news story, when they get to that inevitable 'future of the net' section, mentions the eventual delivery of digital video. So where is it?

> *GNN* decided to find out. This involved short bursts of net surfing followed by long stretches of downloading. (A tip for prospective Internet movie downloaders: develop a time-consuming hobby, like rug weaving.) Fortunately all the searching, and waiting, led to a happy discovery: digital movies are already on the net in growing numbers. True, some of them look like animated postage stamps, but they have the spunky appeal of an embryonic art form.

Installing MPEGPlay

To play movies you get from the Net, you'll need a program that can play MPEG movies. (Although there are some movies in QuickTime format, there are far more MPEG movies. If you're interested in QuickTime, the Viewers page contains a link to download a QuickTime viewer.) To download MPEGPlay, first make a directory for the program. Then return to the NCSA Viewers page and click on the link for MPEGPlay. When the **Save As** dialog appears, save the *.zip* file in the directory. Then quit Windows and unzip the file. To install MPEGPlay into a directory called *MPEG*, type the following at the DOS prompt:

```
PKUNZIP MPEGPLAY.ZIP \WIN32APP\EMOSAIC\MPEG
```

Then add the following lines to the Viewers section of EMOSAIC.INI:

```
TYPE2=video/mpeg
video/mpeg=C:/WIN32APP\EMOSAIC\MPEG\MPEGPLAY.EXE %s
```

Watching Waterfalls

To visit the *Digital Drive-In*, click on the icon on the *GNN Home* page. Among the movies featured in the *Digital Drive-In* is some footage from the Raleigh, North Carolina, *News and Observer's* NandO.net, which integrates video with other information. The *News and Observer* runs a series of features called "Carolina Discoveries," which profile different spots around the state. A story on North Carolina's waterfalls includes two MPEG movies of waterfalls. To see these movies, click on the **GO** button.

This takes you to a page with links to the two movies. This page tells you the format, file size, and length of the clips. "Views of the cascading water" is a 640K MPEG movie that runs 28 seconds, while "The falling waters and the green forest create a tranquil scene" is a 480K MPEG movie that runs 24 seconds.

As Denison notes, getting movies from the Net involves a lot of waiting, so it's usually better to start with smaller clips since they take less time to download. In this example, we'll get the "tranquil scene" video.

When you click on the link, Mosaic asks you to save the movie on your hard disk. When you click **OK**, the download will start.

If you have configured EMOSAIC.INI correctly, MPEGPlay will launch when the file is downloaded and an information window screen will be displayed. Press **Enter** to dismiss this screen and the movie will start playing.

The program will quit when the movie finishes, unless you stop the movie or set it to loop. While we won't give all the details of MPEGPlay, here are some of the operations.

Figure 6-4 shows the MPEGPlay interface with a movie playing. The toolbar has icons to (from right to left) play a movie, advance one frame at a time, stop the movie, restart the movie, and open a file.

The **Dither** menu lets you set the dithering of the playback. As shown in Figure 6-5, the dither options show the number of colors used in each dithering scheme. It's important not to choose an option with more colors than your computer can display. For instance, unless you have a 24-bit color card in your PC, don't choose full-color, because the colors will be way off. You can experiment with the different options to see what works best for each movie.

The **Options** menu lets you set the movie to loop and to stretch to the size of your window. Don't make your window too big or the movie will start to show its pixels. There are also various technical options for video display. See the online documentation (under the **Help** menu) for details on these options.

Digital video is definitely not the big screen. In fact, it's the very small screen. The *News and Observer*'s Eric Harris says: "When it comes to digital video, we're sort of in the black-and-white TV age."

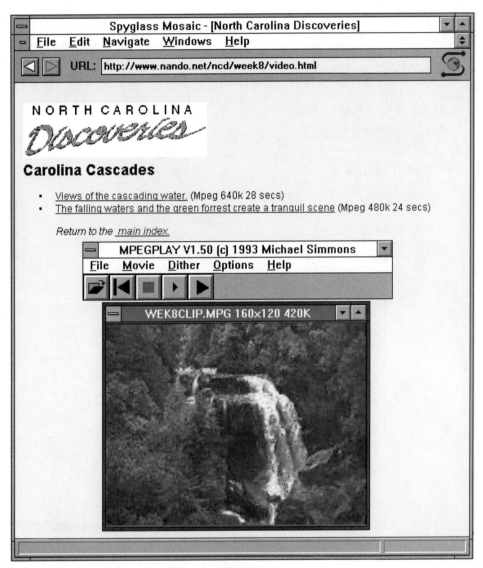

Figure 6–4. Waterfall movie displayed in MPEGView

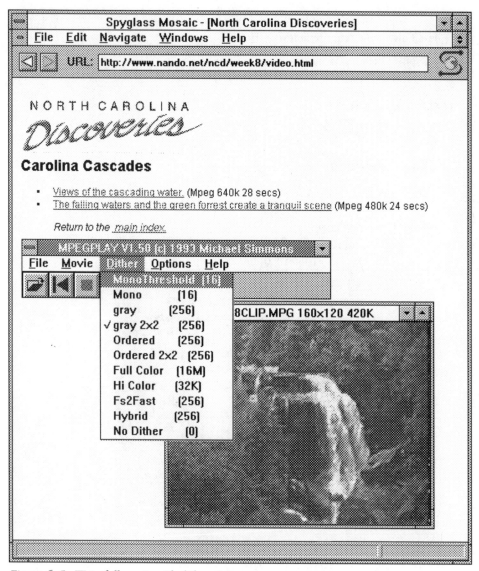

Figure 6-5. Waterfall movie with dither options

Sound Waves

There are all kinds of sounds available on the Internet, from music servers like the Internet Underground Music Archive, the U2 server, and the Elvis server, to sound bytes from Internet Talk Radio and *The Late Show with David Letterman*.

Installing WHAM

There are many different sound file formats, so to play sounds you need a program that supports many different formats. Although it is a fairly complex program, WHAM (Waveform Hold and Modify) does support most of the sound files you're likely to encounter on the Internet.

WHAM offers all kinds of sound editing and playback controls, but the basic controls are as simple as operating a tape deck. In addition to playing sounds, you can cut the sound apart and splice it together in different ways, splice different sounds together, and other nifty stuff. There's only one track, though, so you can't mix sounds together. Detailed operating instructions are available in the online help file.

To download WHAM, make a directory for it. Then go to the NCSA Viewers page and click on the appropriate link. When the **Save As** dialog appears, save the *.zip* file in the appropriate directory. Quit Windows and unzip the file. Depending on how you set up your directories, you'll type something like this at the DOS prompt:

```
PKUNZIP WHAM.ZIP \WIN32APP\EMOSAIC\WHAM
```

To configure Mosaic to launch WHAM when audio files are encountered, enter the following lines in EMOSAIC.INI:

```
TYPE3=audio/basic
audio/basic=C:\WIN32APP\EMOSAIC\WHAM\WHAM.EXE %s
```

Listening to the Underground

One of the most popular music servers on the Internet is the Internet Underground Music Archive, which was awarded a Best of the Net award from *GNN*. "The Net's first free hi-fi music archive," the IUMA is dedicated to promoting unknown and unavailable artists over the Internet.

To use it, click on the Internet Underground Music Archive on the *Mosaic Handbook Hotlist* or enter the IUMA's URL:

```
http://sunsite.unc.edu/ianc/
```

When you get to the IUMA, you'll see one of the hippest home page designs on the Internet, with options to check out bands by artist, label, location, song title, and interactively. You can also select the **Fresh Catches** option to listen to new tracks.

The *Fresh Catches* page describes the music available and provides several links to various versions. There are stereo and mono versions of the whole cut, which typically weigh in at 4 to 5 megabytes, as well as much smaller 15-second samples, which are *.au* files.

Following the smaller-is-better rule of downloading, choose one of the smaller samples. Once again, Mosaic asks you to save the file and then starts the download. There are numerous sound file formats, most of which are supported by WHAM. But it's important to save sound files with the correct extension, so WHAM can play them correctly.

When the file transfer is complete, WHAM launches and displays a waveform of the sound file, as shown in Figure 6-6.

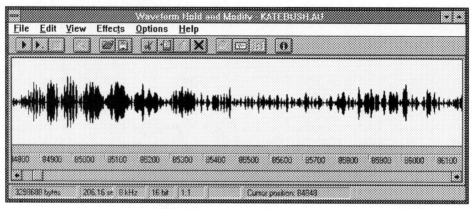

Figure 6-6. Waveform of an audio file

Click on the **Play** button to play the sound or select a portion of the waveform to listen to part of the sound. When you're done, return to Mosaic.

Other Viewers and Files

In this chapter, we've covered some of the basic file formats you may find on the Net. There are other files you will likely encounter, and you'll have to download appropriate viewers for those file types. To help you configure some of these other file types, Table 6-1 shows the MIME types for common file formats.

Table 6-1: Common MIME Types and Subtypes

MIME Type/Subtype	File Format	Appropriate Viewers
image/jpeg	JPEG image	LView
image/gif	GIF image	LView
image/tiff	TIFF image	Paint Shop Pro
audio/basic	Sun *.au* sound files	WHAM
video/mpeg	MPEG video	MPEGPlay
video/quicktime	QuickTime video	QuickTime Viewer
application/postscript	GhostView	

CHAPTER SEVEN

CREATING HTML DOCUMENTS

The Power of Hypertext
The Hypertext Theory of Relativity
Getting Started
Writing HTML
Creating Your Own Home Page
Using HoTMetaL to Create Documents
Resources

So far in this book we've talked about viewing other people's World Wide Web pages. Now we're going to turn the tables and show you how to create your own Web pages. It's not something that requires programming experience or any special skills. All you need is access to a Web server on the Internet (one that uses the HTTP protocol) and the ability to tag text files according to the HTML specification.

Writing HTML documents is actually pretty easy. You can create them using any editor that can save files in plain ASCII text format. Most word processors can write ASCII files, and nearly every text editor writes ASCII files normally.

Unfortunately, there are relatively few tools that help in the process. One of them is Mosaic itself, which lets you preview HTML pages located on your local system. Another is HoTMetaL, a WYSIWYG (what you see is what you get) editor for writing HTML. We'll discuss both of these programs in this chapter.

We'll also go through the standard HTML tags in some detail. While we won't cover every aspect of HTML, we will cover the most common and important tags. You may not be an expert by the time you finish with this chapter, but you will be able to write sophisticated documents for the Web.

The Power of Hypertext

The Web adds a new dimension to writing documents—building hypertext links that connect one document or topic to another. Hypertext is a powerful way to help users navigate through information. To understand just how powerful, think about the way we navigate through printed books. There's a table of contents that describes the content of each chapter; an index that tells you where specific references are located; footnotes and annotations that refer to other sections of the book or to other works; and finally there's the body of the book itself, which (with the exception of mystery novels) people often flip through and scan for information that catches their eye.

Hypertext incorporates all these modes of navigating and adds the instant gratification of seeing a referenced work or section immediately. Within the pages of a hypertext server, an author can point to other pages of general content, point to specific information, let users jump to other works, and let them move through a collection of information in either a linear or nonlinear way.

In many cases, Web documents are multimedia documents with graphics, sound, and video files, as well as text. This presents the author with yet another question—how to combine and present all of these media in a unified document.

Almost all servers have a home page, a front door to the server that provides links to other documents. A home page is a place where you can assert your identity, explain the purpose and scope of your server, and set up links to other documents. Later in this chapter, we'll work on creating your own home page.

The Hypertext Theory of Relativity

HTML is the markup language for World Wide Web documents. A subset of *SGML* (*Standard Generalized Markup Language*), HTML is a standardized language for creating formatted hypertext documents. It lets you perform two main tasks: defining hypertext anchors and links, and describing the format of the document.

Formatting is defined only in rather general, often relative terms. HTML does not tell Mosaic, for example, "Make this line 36 point Palatino." It simply identifies the text as a heading, and Mosaic uses that description to format and display the text.

The reason that HTML describes documents in general rather than specific terms is that there is no single World Wide Web browser that everyone uses. There are several different browsers, and more are likely to be developed in the future. What they have in common is that they are all able to display HTML documents. But they all do it differently.

The differences between browsers tend to reflect the limitations of different computing environments. For instance, Mosaic runs in a graphical user interface, so it can display graphics, type styles, and point sizes. Lynx is for character-based environments, so it makes do with more limited formatting capabilities. Some future computer platform might translate all text into spoken words, and a browser for that system might read plain text in a calm voice and headings in hearty yells.

In addition, not all users have the same set of fonts, so a document that specifies Palatino for headlines might use Courier on a system that doesn't include Palatino. That's a common problem when PC users try to share files, and it's one that HTML avoids by leaving the formatting to the browser.

The basic philosophy of HTML is that authors need not be concerned with the way the document will look; that's the job of the browser. If the file is tagged correctly, each browser will display the document to the best of its abilities.

Getting Started

You already have the most important tool for writing HTML—Mosaic itself. You can use Mosaic to preview documents on your local system by using the **Open Local** command. This works just like the **Open** command in any Windows program: it launches a dialog box that lets you open a file on your computer. Since you're working on local files, this is one time you don't have to be on the network to use Mosaic.

You can also access local files with the **Open URL** command. In this case, you need to use the following syntax:

```
File:///c:/dir/subdir/filename
```

Note that the URL uses slashes, not backslashes as DOS and Windows do.

As we go through examples in this chapter, you can try writing your own HTML documents and previewing them in Mosaic. Remember to save your work as text files and to use the extension *.htm.*

NOTE

One confusing thing about writing HTML documents on DOS and Windows computers is the filename limitation. Filenames in DOS and Windows can have no more than 11 characters, and file extensions can have no more than three characters. Thus, you should save your HTML documents with an extension of *.htm.* However, most documents on the Web have extensions of *.html,* since UNIX accepts much longer filenames than DOS. We assume that you will eventually move your documents to a UNIX machine for publication on the Web. At this point, you should rename your documents with the *.html* extension for the sake of consistency with other Web documents. (If your documents will actually be served on a DOS computer, you'll have to leave the *.htm* filenames.) In this chapter, we will use the *.html* extension, even though you will initially save files as *.htm.*

Let's take a look at a real-world document. Here is the HTML document that describes the *What's Up in GNN* page:

```
<HTML><HEAD>
<TITLE>What's Up in GNN</TITLE>
</HEAD><BODY>
<A HREF="/gnn/wel/welcome.html">
<IMG ALT="Global Network Navigator--Charting the Internet"
SRC="/gnn/graphics/HOME.gif"></A>
<P>
<IMG ALT="What's Up?" SRC="/gnn/graphics/WU.xbm">
```

```
<UL>
<LI>The
<A HREF="/gnn/meta/finance/index.html">Personal Finance Center</A>
brings readers
<A HREF="/gnn/meta/finance/feat/foreclosure.html"><B>Real Estate
Foreclosures</B></A>,
a feature article from the Brookfield Economics Institute
discussing the "ins and outs" of foreclosure for buyers and sellers
alike.
<P>
</BODY></HTML>
```

If that looks discouraging, don't worry. It's really not that bad. In fact, once you get the vocabulary down, HTML is quite a simple beast to master. As you can see from the *GNN* example above, you can create highly sophisticated documents using HTML.

There are three basic conventions of the HTML language, and once you understand them, writing HTML is a breeze. These conventions are tags, attributes, and URLs.

Tags

The most basic element in an HTML document is a tag, which is usually bracketed by the "less than" and "greater than" signs, < and >. Tags often come in pairs and surround text, much like quotation marks, with one tag starting the action and another tag ending it. Ending tags look just like starting tags except for a slash mark preceding the tag name within the brackets. For instance, <H1> is the starting tag for a top-level headline and </H1> is the ending tag. Here's a simple example of how tags are used in HTML:

```
<TITLE>This is the title</TITLE>
<H1>This is a headline</H1>
This is plain text.
```

Some tags work by themselves without ending tags. These tags usually identify special characters or tell the browser to insert something. For instance, the tag & represents the ampersand (&). Often tags are nested inside one another. Some tags accept nesting while others do not. Nesting is often used with lists to create an outline format.

Finally, tags are exclusive, not additive. Two tags can't be added together to create a hybrid effect. Each tag has its own formatting, completely independent of nearby tags. For instance, if you have a sentence in italic (using the <I> tag) and want to put a word or two in bold italic, you might think that just placing the bold tags (<B> and </B>) around the words would work:

```
<I>An italic sentence with <B>bold-italic </B>type.</I>
```

It doesn't. Each subsequent tag supersedes the previous tags, so you get regular bold, not bold-italic:

> *An italic sentence with* **bold-italic** *type.*

Combining the tags (<BI>) doesn't work for the same reason. In fact, there really is no way to call out bold-italic type in HTML.

Attributes

With some tags, you need to use attributes to define exactly how the action will work. These attributes vary from tag to tag. They are like multiple-choice questions; there are several possible answers, or values, for each attribute. The syntax for using attributes is:

```
<TAG ATTRIBUTE="VALUE">
```

In this chapter, we'll talk about the most important attributes for each of the tags, but we won't necessarily cover all of them. Refer to Appendix B, *HTML Reference Guide*, for more information about these attributes.

URLs

Attributes are often used to specify files as links. To specify a file, use the document's URL as the value of an attribute. For example, IMG, the tag used to include a graphic or figure, takes the attribute SRC (for "source") to indicate which file to use. In this case, the document's URL is the value of SRC:

```
<IMG SRC="http://gnn.com/graphics/HOME.gif">
```

For a more detailed discussion of URLs, see Chapter 2, *Getting Started with Mosaic.*

Writing HTML

There are two steps in creating a page for the Web—formatting the document and building links to other files. To get started, let's go through a simple HTML document. Below is the HTML document for the home page of a fictional server about the Marx Brothers comedy team. Figure 7-1 shows how the page appears in Mosaic.

```
<HTML>
<HEAD>
<TITLE>The Marx Brothers Home Page</TITLE></HEAD>
<BODY>
<H1>The Marx Brothers Web Server</H1>
Welcome Marx Brothers Fans!
<HR>
Get Information About The Brothers By Clicking On Their Names:
<P><A HREF="groucho.html">GROUCHO</A>
<P><A HREF="harpo.html">HARPO</A>
```

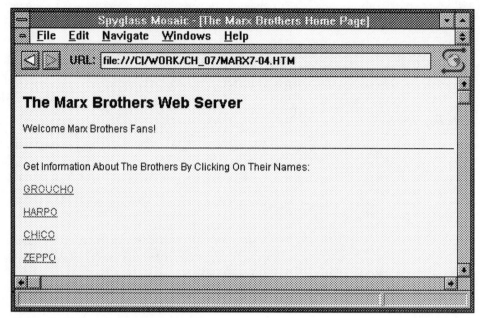

Figure 7–1. Marx Brothers home page

```
<P><A HREF="chico.html">CHICO</A>
<P><A HREF="zeppo.html">ZEPPO</A>
</BODY></HTML>
```

Identification Tags

An HTML document consists of several tags that give information to the browser but don't actually affect the content. These tags give the title of the document and tell the browser when the header starts and ends, when the body starts and ends, and so on.

Document identifier tag

    `<HTML>` and `</HTML>`

The Marx Brothers document opens with the `<HTML>` tag. `<HTML>` is the opening tag for all Web documents. It tells the Web browser that this is in fact an HTML document and not some other structured document. `</HTML>` marks the end of the document. Note that everything else in the document is nested inside these two tags. In fact, Mosaic and most other browsers do not insist on the use of these tags, but using them may prove to be more important in the future.

Header

> <HEAD> and </HEAD>

While there are actually several elements that can be included in the header, the only important one is the title.

Title

> <TITLE> and </TITLE>

The title is the name of the document as it appears in the browser's title window, history list, and hotlist. The title tag is part of the header, so it needs to be within the two header tags.

There are a few technical rules worth mentioning here:

- There may only be one title in any document.

- The title cannot contain anchors (explained later), paragraph marks, or text formatting.

- The title is not normally displayed in the text of a document itself, although the opening heading could consist of the same text as the title.

- While there is technically no limit to the length of a title, it's a good idea to keep it less than 64 characters. This is because some browsers may truncate it in window titles, menus, and hotlists.

- Each document within the collection of documents should have a unique title.

- The title should describe the page out of context. That is, it should refer to the whole collection of documents, not just a specific document. You can imagine how confusing it would be if you followed a hypertext link only to arrive at a page labeled merely "Home Page."

In the following example, the title is nested within the header tags, which in turn are nested within the document identifier tags. The ellipsis represents the body of the document, which is itself nested within the HTML tags.

```
<HTML>
     <HEAD>
          <TITLE>The Marx Brothers Home Page
          </TITLE>
     </HEAD>
       . . .
</HTML>
```

Body identifier

`<BODY>` and `</BODY>`

We're almost ready to start writing the document, but there is one more technical item. The `<BODY>` tag indicates that we're ready to start the actual document. Now, you might think that since we explicitly ended the header, the Web browser would be able to tell where the body starts, but HTML calls for an explicit tag to start the body. In fact, Mosaic and other browsers don't insist on the use of the body tag, but again, it's a good practice and may be important to future browsers.

Crafting the Page: Formatting Text

HTML provides several ways to control the presentation of text on the screen. While it doesn't provide precise control over the placement of text and graphics, it does enable you to specify a great deal about the way your page is structured.

Headings

`<H1>` and `</H1>` ... `<H6>` and `</H6>`

There are six levels of headings, with `<H1>` having the most emphasis and `<H6>` having the least. Exactly how these headings are displayed is up to the different browsers. Mosaic displays `<H1>` in large bold text, while Lynx puts the header text in all caps and centers it. The other header elements, `<H2>` through `<H6>`, are of gradually reduced emphasis.

Don't use header elements below `<H3>`, because the display of these minor levels is notoriously inconsistent between browsers; a small but readable header in one browser may be indecipherable in another. More importantly, if you feel the need to have more than three levels of information, consider breaking the document up into several smaller documents and linking the documents to each other. Each document could then have its own `<H1>` element.

In the following example, we've added the body tag, an `<H1>` header, and some plain text. The text between the `<H1>` tags is the first thing the user will see. Viewed in Mosaic, it will be the biggest text on the page. `<H1>` indicates the start of the heading text and `</H1>` indicates the end of it. The next line of text has no formatting codes, so it is presented as regular text. Figure 7-2 is a screen shot of this page in Mosaic.

```
<HTML>
<HEAD>
<TITLE>The Marx Brothers Home Page
</TITLE>
</HEAD>
<BODY>
<H1>The Marx Brothers Web Server
</H1>
Welcome Marx Brothers fans!
```

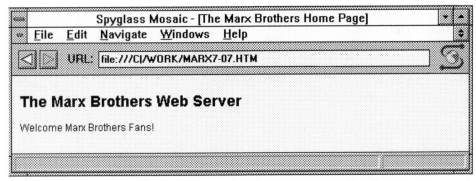

Figure 7–2. Document with an <H1> heading and plain text viewed in Mosaic

Breaking paragraphs and lines

As far as HTML is concerned, the only thing you can do with a keyboard is type text. It does not respond to even rudimentary formatting techniques, such as entering carriage returns or extra spaces. To format text, even to indicate the beginning of a new paragraph, you must use tags. In this section, we'll discuss the tags that let you control the structure of text on the page. Note that these tags do not require ending tags.

Paragraphs <P>

The paragraph tag starts a new paragraph. Since carriage returns are ignored, you could simply place paragraph tags at the appropriate place in a block of text, like this:

```
Paragraph one.<P>Paragraph two.<P>Paragraph three.
```

or you could insert returns to make it easier for you to visualize the page, like this:

```
Paragraph one.
<P>
Paragraph two.
<P>
Paragraph three.
```

The result would be the same—three separate paragraphs. Exactly how those paragraphs would be displayed would, of course, be up to the individual browsers. Most browsers insert space after a paragraph, so there's no need for more than one paragraph tag. In fact you'll want to keep an eye out for redundant paragraph tags, as some browsers (Lynx, for instance) will insert space for every paragraph tag. Mosaic, on the other hand, ignores extra paragraph tags.

Line Breaks

What do you do if you want to break a line but you don't want to start a new paragraph? Simple. Use <BR> for a line break. This tag starts a new line but doesn't format a new paragraph. It is commonly used to format a block of text, such as an address:

```
Name<BR>
Address<BR>
Phone Number
<P>
```

Rules <HR>

To make a horizontal rule, don't make the mistake of just typing a bunch of under-line characters. Because various browsers may be set up for different line widths, this may create unattractive effects for some users. Instead, use <HR>. It causes a paragraph break and draws a horizontal rule across the screen.

In the following example, we've added paragraph tags, line break tags, and a hori-zontal rule to the Marx Brothers Home Page. Figure 7-3 shows the display of this document in Mosaic. There are three separate paragraphs on this page. Note that no paragraph tag is used before the horizontal rule because the <HR> tag automati-cally starts a new paragraph.

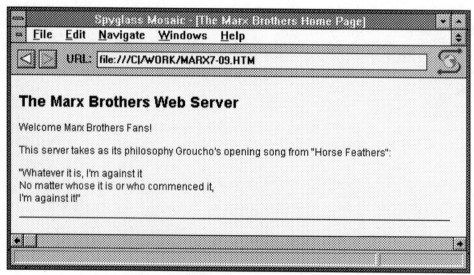

Figure 7-3. Document with paragraphs, line breaks, and horizontal rule

```
<HTML>
<HEAD>
<TITLE>The Marx Brothers Home Page</TITLE>
</HEAD>
<BODY>
<H1>The Marx Brothers Web Server</H1>
Welcome Marx Brothers fans!
<P>This server takes as its philosophy Groucho's opening song from
"Horse Feathers":
<P>"Whatever it is, I'm against it<BR>
No matter whose it is or who commenced it,<BR>
I'm against it!"
<HR>
```

Lists and glossaries

The list and glossary tags can be powerful because they allow for fairly sophisticated formatting through simple tags. Lists are a good illustration of the power of HTML because they let the author generally indicate the nature of the information, while the browsers take care of the exact format.

Lists are simply paragraphs, sentences, phrases, or single words presented in an itemized format. There are several kinds of lists. The most commonly used ones are ordered lists and unordered lists. Glossaries have a structure in which each item is a term followed by a definition. The terms are usually short items, while the definitions can be several paragraphs in length. Both glossaries and lists can be nested.

Lists

Entries in unordered lists are preceded by bullets. Entries in ordered lists are preceded by numbers in ascending order. Lists start with an opening tag (<UL> for unordered lists, <OL> for ordered lists) and end with a closing tag. Each item in the list is preceded by the <LI> tag, which does not require a closing tag. The syntax for an unordered list is:

```
<UL>
<LI>Text
<LI>Text
</UL>
```

This example shows an unordered list in HTML, and Figure 7-4 shows the list displayed in Mosaic.

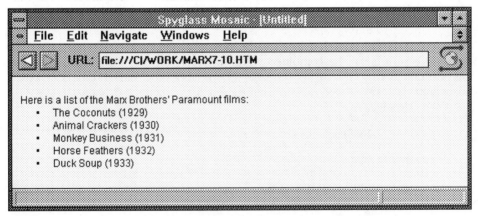

Figure 7-4. An unordered list viewed in Mosaic

```
Here is a list of the Marx Brothers' Paramount films:
<UL>
<LI>The Coconuts (1929)
<LI>Animal Crackers (1930)
<LI>Monkey Business (1931)
```

```
<LI>Horse Feathers (1932)
<LI>Duck Soup (1933)
</UL>
```

The syntax is very similar for ordered lists, with just the opening and closing tags changing:

```
<OL>
<LI>Text
<LI>Text
</OL>
```

Figure 7-5 shows what the previous example looks like in Mosaic if we use an ordered list instead of an unordered one.

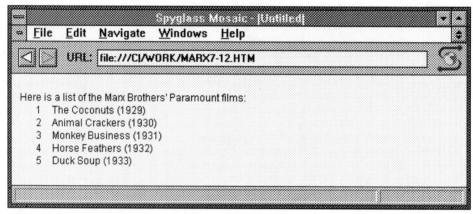

Figure 7-5. An ordered list viewed in Mosaic

Both ordered and unordered lists can be nested to create an outline format, and both kinds of lists can be combined within a larger list. For instance, the following example gives a table of contents for a book about the Marx Brothers in which unordered lists are nested within an ordered list. Figure 7-6 shows the list as viewed in Mosaic.

```
<H1>Table of Contents</H1>
<OL>
<LI>Vaudeville Days
        <UL>
        <LI>Fun in Hi Skule
        <LI>Mr. Green's Reception
        <LI>Home Again
        </UL>
<LI>On Broadway
        <UL>
        <LI>I'll Say She Is (1924)
        <LI>The Coconuts (1925)
        <LI>Animal Crackers (1928)
```

```
        </UL>
<LI>The Paramount Films
        <UL>
        <LI>The Coconuts (1929)
        <LI>Animal Crackers (1930)
        <LI>Monkey Business (1931)
        <LI>Horse Feathers (1932)
        <LI>Duck Soup (1933)
        </UL>
</OL>
```

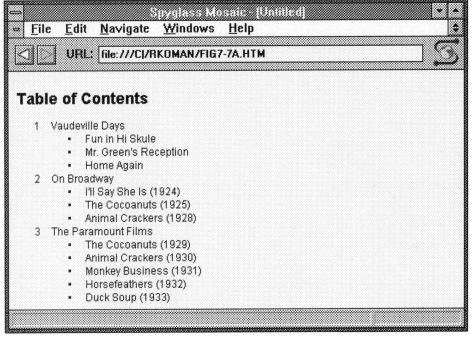

Figure 7–6. Table of Contents with nested lists, viewed in Mosaic

Glossaries

As mentioned earlier, glossaries consist of terms, which are usually short, and longer descriptions, which are indented in Mosaic. Glossaries use four tags:

- <DL> to start the glossary

- <DT> for the main entry or term

- <DD> for the descriptive paragraph, or definition

- </DL> to end the glossary

The syntax is:

```
<DL>
<DT>Term One
<DD>Definition of Term One.
<DT>Term Two
<DD>Definition of Term Two.
</DL>
```

The following example gives the HTML for a two-item glossary. Figure 7-7 shows how the glossary is presented in Mosaic.

```
<H2>Marx Brothers Film Summaries</H2>
<DL>
<DT>"The Coconuts" (1929)
<DD>Their first film, for Paramount, puts the brothers in Florida during
the land boom of the 1920s. It features the famous "Why a Duck?" routine
with Groucho and Chico.
<DT>"Animal Crackers" (1930)
<DD>Like "The Coconuts," based on a Broadway show of the same name,
"Animal Crackers" features Groucho as Captain Spaulding, the African explorer.
<P>It boasts the classic line: "One morning I shot an elephant in my pajamas.
How he got in my pajamas, I don't know."
</DL>
```

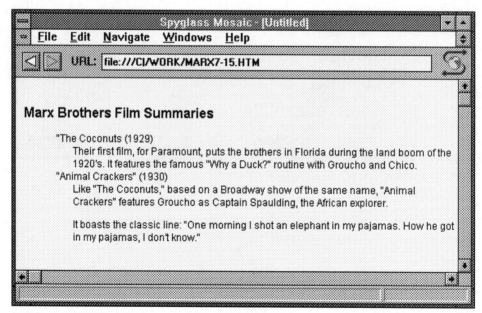

Figure 7-7. HTML glossary as viewed in Mosaic

Note that <P> can be used within definitions to create multiple paragraphs. Other formatting tags, except the heading tags, can also be used. You can nest ordered and unordered lists within a glossary. For example, you could include an outline (which could include many nested lists) within a glossary definition.

Text attributes

```
<EM> and </EM>
<STRONG> and </STRONG>
<B> and </B>
<I> and </I>
<U> and </U>
```

There are two kinds of tags for text attributes in HTML—physical styles (bold, italic, underline) and logical styles, which let the author format based on his intentions rather than having to specify the exact look of the text. The primary logical styles are <EM> (for emphasized text) and <STRONG> (for even more emphasized text). The idea is that emphasized text is visually louder than plain text and stronger text is louder still, as shown below:

```
This is very important: <EM>Always lock the door when you leave.</EM>
<STRONG>Always.</STRONG>
```

Figure 7-8 shows how this is presented in Mosaic.

Figure 7-8. EM and STRONG types viewed in Mosaic

As a rule, you should use <EM> and <STRONG> instead of the physical styles (<B>, <I>, and <U>). This is because every browser understands these tags and interprets them in a relative, rather than absolute, way. That is, while different browsers display <EM> and <STRONG> differently, they will all display <EM> text as louder than plain text and <STRONG> text as louder than <EM> text.

In X Mosaic and Windows Mosaic, text tagged with <EM> displays in italic, and text tagged as <STRONG> displays in bold. Mac Mosaic underlines the emphasized text and puts strong text in bold. Lynx underlines emphasized text and does the same for strong text.

As for underlining—don't. Underlined text is too easily confused with hypertext links, which are often underlined.

Preformatted text

<PRE> and </PRE>

Sometimes you want to control exactly the way text will look. You can do that (within limitations) by using the <PRE> tag. Preformatted text always appears in a monospaced font like Courier, and unlike with other HTML text, carriage returns and extra spaces work. For these reasons, many people use preformatted text for tables, like this:

```
<PRE>
Title                   Date
A Night at the Opera    1937
A Day at the Races      1938
At the Circus           1939
Go West                 1940
The Big Store           1941
</PRE>
```

You can use most other tags, including hypertext links, within preformatted text.

Address format

<ADDRESS> and </ADDRESS>

This tag was originally intended as a format for contact information at the bottom of a page, but you can use it whenever you want to set a paragraph such as a date apart from the rest of the page. Text appears in italics.

Special characters

What do you do when you want to use characters that have special meanings in HTML? There are four such characters:

- < (the left angle bracket)

- > (the right angle bracket)

- & (ampersand)

- " (quote marks)

HTML includes character combinations, called escape sequences, to represent these characters in an HTML document. They are:

- < (the escape sequence for <)

- > (the escape sequence for >)

- & (the escape sequence for &)

- " (the escape sequence for ")

It is important to note that escape sequences are case-sensitive, unlike all other HTML tags. There are many more escape sequences for non-ASCII characters. Some of the more common ones are:

- ö (the escape sequence for a lowercase o with an umlaut)

- ñ (the escape sequence for a lowercase n with a tilde)

- È (the escape sequence for an uppercase E with a grave accent)

Weaving Threads: Anchor Links

    <A> and </A>

Now for the fun part—creating anchors and hypertext links. As discussed earlier, links are the way that users are guided through a body of hypertext information. In the parlance of HTML, an anchor is the hypertext itself—the element that the user selects in order to go to the linked document. An anchor can be a word, a phrase, a picture, an icon, or anything that can be displayed on an HTML page. The linked item, that is, the place the user goes after clicking on the anchor, can be any file—not just another HTML document, but also a Gopher menu, a WAIS database, an FTP site, etc. For the sake of simplicity, however, we'll talk primarily about linking HTML documents together.

Linking to other documents

By now you're quite familiar with how to recognize and use hypertext links. In this section, you'll learn how to create them. We'll start by discussing how to link to other documents on your computer; then we'll move on to linking to other documents on the Internet.

You'll probably start out writing your documents on your PC, but at some point, you'll need to move your files over to an HTTP server to make them available on the Web. For that reason, it's a good idea to use only filenames in your links, not directory names, since your files will have a different path on the server than they do on your PC.

The first step is to create an anchor, which you do with the anchor tag <A>, and the HREF attribute. The anchor tag tells the browser, "Make the following text a hypertext anchor," and HREF tells it, "Link the anchor to this file." Here's the syntax:

```
<A HREF="filename">HYPERTEXT</A>
```

Consider the original Marx Brothers home page shown in Figure 7-10. The mouse is positioned over the word **GROUCHO**, which is displayed as a hypertext anchor. At the bottom of the screen Mosaic displays the name of the file that is linked to

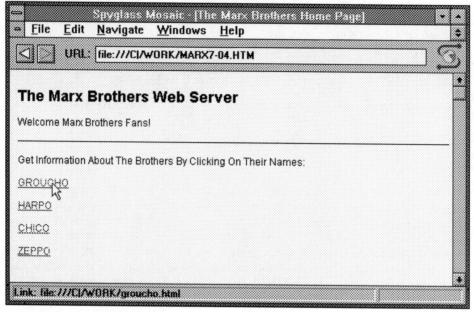

Figure 7–9. Hypertext links displayed in status bar in Mosaic

this anchor. Here is the HTML that causes Mosaic to display **GROUCHO** as a hypertext anchor.

```
<A HREF="groucho.html">Groucho</A>
```

This line says: Make the word **GROUCHO** an anchor that links to the file *groucho.html*. In this case, the file is on the same computer and in the same directory as the active page, so we only gave the filename. But we could link to a file in another directory on the same computer, or to another computer on the Internet.

Let's add to this page a hypertext anchor that links to a document on another server. To do this, we need to give the URL of the linked file. The hypertext will say, "Learn more about the 1930s," and will link to the home page of a collection of documents about the 1930s that exists on a computer called **college.edu**. Here's the HTML:

```
<A HREF="http://college.edu/USHistory/1930s/HomePage.html">Learn
more about the 1930s</A>
```

When users click on the anchor, they are connected to **college.edu** and the linked page is displayed.

When creating links, remember that you can link to any file, not just an HTML page. You can create links to video, audio, graphic, or CAD files. The only proviso is that users need to have external viewers to handle these files, so you'll probably want to stick to the common formats.

Naming anchors

Another feature of the anchor tag is the ability to name anchors. This is a helpful navigation technique for large documents. By linking to a named anchor, you can take the user right to a specific part of the page, as illustrated in Figure 7-10. While, in theory, you could link to a named anchor on another server, it's much more common to use names within your own server or within a single page.

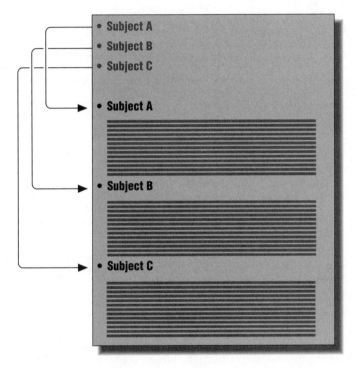

Figure 7–10. Hypertext used to link to text within a document

Let's say you want to set up an anchor to link **GROUCHO** to an essay later in the same page. The first step is to set up a name for the linked text, using the NAME attribute with the <A> tag. The syntax is:

```
<A NAME="name">TEXT</A>
```

Here's how we would name the essay about Groucho:

```
<A NAME="grouchobio"><B>Groucho Marx: A Life</B></A><P>
Groucho Marx was famous for quick wit, a greasepaint mustache and
eyebrows, and a big cigar. He and his brothers were the preeminent comedians
of film in the 1930s. While Harpo and Chico made a legendary slapstick duo,
often quoting the vocabulary of vaudeville and burlesque in their routines,
Groucho was without doubt the star of the show. The Marx Brothers started
in burlesque and by the mid-20s were the toast of New York in the Broadway
shows "The Coconuts" and "Animal Crackers." Those plays were brought to the
screen as very early talkies in 1929 and 1930. Their film career was
effectively over by the early `40s but Groucho managed a comeback as host of
the game show "You Bet Your Life" in the 1950s.
```

Note that we only named the title of the essay, but we could have named the entire essay, since it is fairly short. Since the hypertext anchor will take us to the beginning of the essay, there's really no point in naming the entire thing.

Now that we've named the paragraph, we can link to it from earlier in the page:

```
Welcome Marx Brothers fans!
<HR>
Get information about the brothers by clicking on their names:
<P><A HREF="#grouchobio"> Groucho</A>
```

The last line of the above code now says: Make **GROUCHO** an anchor and, when the user clicks on it, link to the text named "grouchobio." Note that you use # to specify the name as a link.

Any text can be named, even another anchor. Remember that **NAME** is an attribute, just like **HREF**. Here's the syntax for naming text that is also a hypertext anchor:

```
<A HREF="linked file" NAME="name">Hypertext anchor</A>
```

Inserting graphics

```
<IMG>
```

The combination of graphics and text is one of the things that make the World Wide Web so interesting. In our Marx Brothers server, we could include photos of the brothers, stills from their films, and so on.

There are two ways to present graphics in the World Wide Web—inline graphics (those that appear within the page) and linked graphics (stand-alone files reached by links). HTML only supports the XBM and GIF file formats for inline graphics; however, if you link to a graphics file, it can be in any format—provided that users have the external viewers with which to view them. The most common file formats are JPEG and GIF; it's probably a good idea to convert graphics to one of those formats. (Chapter 6 has more information about file formats and viewers.)

The tag for inserting an inline graphic is <IMG>. Since the tag doesn't refer to text, there's no end tag involved. This tag always requires a source attribute (SRC), which defines the name of the file to insert. The value for the SRC attribute can be any URL. The URL can point to a GIF or XBM file on any computer on the Internet, although it's probably safer to maintain inline graphics files locally, just in case the other computer is inaccessible.

There are two other attributes that can be included in the tag:

- ALIGN specifies how graphics and/or text should align. The values are TOP, MIDDLE, and BOTTOM. They tell the browser to align nearby text with the top, middle, or bottom of the graphic.

- ALT defines some alternate text to be used in case a browser cannot display graphics. This is important for users of non-graphical browsers such as Lynx. If the graphic is an integral part of your content, you'll want to be sure to specify some alternate text.

Let's say we want to insert a photo of Groucho before his name and have the accompanying text line up with the bottom of the image. For Lynx users, we'll display the phrase "[Photo of Groucho Marx]." Here's the tag:

```
<IMG SRC="groucho.gif" ALIGN=BOTTOM ALT="[Photo of Groucho Marx]">
```

Inserting graphics as anchors

We can also insert a graphic and make it an anchor for a hypertext link. Here the photo of Groucho is an anchor to the specified file:

```
<A HREF="marxbros.html"><IMG SRC="groucho.gif" ALIGN=BOTTOM></A>
```

One common use of graphics as anchors is for custom bullets. Instead of using an unordered list, which uses bullets, you can put postage-stamp size graphics in front of text and have them do double duty as custom bullets and hypertext links. It's a good way to give your page some personality. If you wanted to use a picture of Groucho as a linked bullet, for instance, you might write:

```
<P><A HREF="file1.html"><IMG SRC="groucho.gif" ALIGN=BOTTOM></A>Information
about Groucho's life
<P><A HREF="file2.html"><IMG SRC="groucho.gif" ALIGN=BOTTOM></A>Information
about Groucho's family
<P><A HREF="file3.html"><IMG SRC="groucho.gif" ALIGN=BOTTOM></A>Information
about Groucho's work
```

Figure 7-11 shows how this list looks in Mosaic.

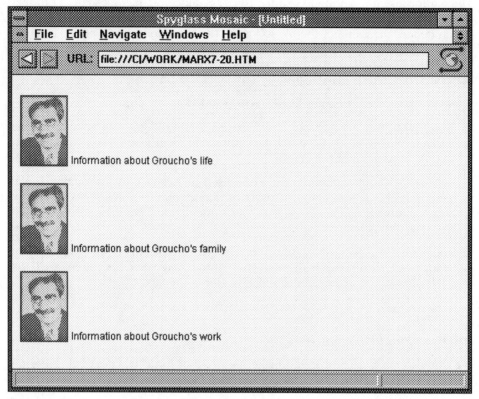

Figure 7–11. Custom bullets used as hypertext anchors

Creating Your Own Home Page

If first impressions really are the most important, you'll want to pay particular attention to your home page. The home page is the first document users come to when they contact your server. It introduces users to your service, tells them what kind of information they'll find, and provides links to documents on your server or others. Beyond that there really are no rules for home pages. Companies, colleges, publications, scientists, students . . . they all have Web servers on the Internet, with very different home pages. In this section, we'll take a look at some of the different home pages out there and discuss how you can make the right impression.

A personal home page occupies a unique niche on the World Wide Web: it represents the Web at its most basic and at its most eccentric. We can lay the blame for this multiple-personality disorder on evolution. From its simple text-based roots in CERN, the WWW home page has rapidly grown into a flexible self-publishing tool. It can now serve as anything from a conservative, professional-looking front door on the Net, to a medium of personal expression that intersects with autobiography, e-zines, and science fiction.

What should you put in your home page? Here are a few thoughts about different approaches (with the linked servers shown in brackets), taken from *GNN*'s *Netizens* feature, written by D.C. Denison:

Be Professional:

I graduated from Utah State University [USU] with a degree in Music [Internet Underground Music Archives], and now I work with the Global Network Navigator [GNN].

Wax Literary:

It was a dark and stormy night [weather server]. Nancy Drew leaned back in her trusty '62 T-bird [rec.auto.classic] and turned the radio dial to KKSF [SF radio station Web site].

Get Up Close and Personal:

I live with an amazing standard poodle named Willie [picture of Willie], and love to ponder the meaning of life [philosophy gopher] while watching basketball [GNN Sports Page].

Be an Information Kiosk:

Here is a list of all the free Mac software on the Net [Internet Computer Index], all the online guides to cyberspace [GNN Gold Mine], and a list of all the Internet bicycle information [cycling gopher].

The attitude you decide on will tell you a lot about the other aspects of designing your page. If you're creating a professional page, you'll want your photograph to be professional and your links to be clearly identified. If you're being more personal, you can embed lots of links within text, make inside jokes, show off your homemade computer art, and so on.

To help you get started with that first home page, here are a couple of templates. All you need to do is fill in the blanks, and you're off and running. This template is the HTML for a generic personal home page. It uses an inline image, unordered lists, and some links, as well as the <ADDRESS> tag.

```
<HTML><HEAD>
<TITLE>YourName's Home Page</TITLE></HEAD><BODY>
<H1>YourName's Home Page</H1>
<IMG SRC="YourPicture.gif"> picture title
<H2>Where I work/go to school</H2>
I work at <A HREF="URL here">company/school name</A>.
<H2>Hobbies</H2>
<UL>
<LI>description
<LI>description
<LI>description
</UL>
<H2>Personal Hot List</H2>
<UL>
<LI><A HREF="URL here">description</A>
<LI><A HREF="URL here">description</A>
```

```
<LI><A HREF="URL here">description</A>
</UL>
<ADDRESS>YourName (YourEmailAddress@host.domain) </ADDRESS>
</BODY></HTML>
```

You can fill this out and use it as your home page or customize it as you wish. Figure 7-12 shows a filled-out version of this page.

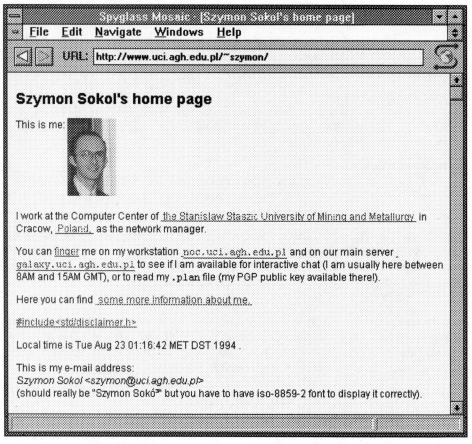

Figure 7–12. Personal home page

The following template is a somewhat more complex form, featuring custom bullets in glossaries, as well as inline images and plenty of links. Try filling out this template and previewing the results in Mosaic.

```
<HTML><HEAD>
<TITLE>My Favorite Things</TITLE></HEAD>
<BODY>
<H1>These Are a Few of My Favorite Things</H1>
This page is all about the things I like.
```

```
<DL>
<DT>
<IMG ALIGN=BOTTOM SRC="picture.gif">
<A HREF="startrek.html">Star Trek: The Next Generation</A>
<DD>
<I>My all time favorite TV show</I>
<DT>
<IMG ALIGN=BOTTOM SRC="picture.gif">
<A HREF="bogart.html">Casablanca</A>
<DD>
<I>My all time favorite movie</I>
<DT>
<IMG ALIGN=BOTTOM SRC="pics/whiteball.gif">
<A HREF="ulysses.html">Ulysses by James Joyce</A>
<DD>
<I>My all time favorite book</I>
</DL>
</BODY></HTML>
```

Using HoTMetaL to Create Documents

While HTML is a relatively simple tagging language, it is easy to make mistakes. If you miss an end tag somewhere, your whole document may be displayed in bold or as <H3> text. If the mistake occurs in a large document, it may be rather difficult to find and correct. At the very least, your fingers will get tired from typing out all those tags.

One solution is a new program called HoTMetaL, available in both freeware and commercial versions. There is a link for downloading HoTMetaL on the *Mosaic Handbook Hotlist,* or you can download it yourself using the URL *ftp://ftp.ncsa.uiuc.edu/Web/html/hotmetal/Windows/hotmetal.exe.* Developed by SoftQuad for X and for Windows, HoTMetaL solves some of the problems of writing HTML from scratch. For starters, the **Insert** pull-down menu gives you a list of all the tags, so you don't have to keep them all in your head.

In addition, HoTMetaL is a rules-based program, so it won't let you make any boneheaded mistakes. For instance, whenever you insert a tag, say <H1>, HoTMetaL automatically inserts the appropriate ending tag. All of this saves you from the endless typing of tags. In fact, HoTMetaL's rules are a good bit stricter than they currently need to be, since Mosaic and other browsers are fairly forgiving of documents that don't adhere to the letter of the law. For this reason, HoTMetaL gives you the option of turning off the rules. As the program's manual notes, however, future browsers are likely to be more insistent on proper tagging, so it's a good idea to use HoTMetaL's rules.

HoTMetaL is more than just a fancy macro program; it's also a WYSIWYG editor. Titles, headers, and other tagged text are displayed in different fonts and point sizes to give you an idea of what the document looks like as you're writing it. The display of all tags is configurable by the user.

Another strong point of this freeware program is that it allows you to save templates, which is useful if you have many documents with a similar structure. Figure 7-13 is a screen shot of the HoTMetaL interface.

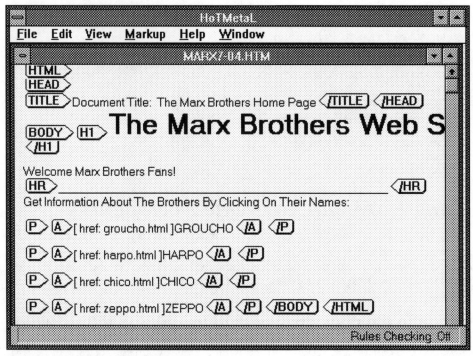

Figure 7-13. The HoTMetaL interface

Marking Up

The primary menu is the **Markup** menu, which lets you insert and edit HTML tags. To get started, you use the **Insert Element** command to bring up a scrolling box of possible tags. By selecting one of the tags, you insert both the opening tag and the closing tag. If you try to insert an element with the cursor positioned where no tags are allowed, HoTMetaL disables the **Insert Element** command. This dialog box also has a checkbox labeled **Include Required Elements**. When this is checked, sub-elements to a tag are automatically inserted along with the tag. For instance, inserting <HTML> automatically inserts <HEAD> as well.

You can edit the attributes and URLs of an element by using the **Edit Attributes and Links** command. Select an element and then choose this command from the **Markup** menu. This brings up a dialog box with the name of each attribute and either a drop-down menu with possible values or a text box for specifying a name of some kind. For instance, if you select an IMG tag, the dialog box will show the ALIGN attribute with the choices TOP, MIDDLE, BOTTOM. Simply select another choice and the element is edited. The dialog box also has text fields for editing the URLs specified with HREF or SRC.

The **Surround** command lets you select text and then surround it with a tag. For instance, you might decide to change a line from plain text to an <H3> heading. To do this, select the text, choose **Surround**, and then pick H3 from the menu. HoTMetaL will put an <H3> tag before the text and </H3> after it.

Rules Checking

HoTMetaL prevents markup errors essentially by removing temptation. The program presents a restricted list of tags, so that only correct tags are available from the **Insert Element** dialog box. This list changes according to the element within which the cursor is positioned. In addition, HoTMetaL disables commands that would cause the document to be incorrectly coded. If at any point this all gets too restrictive, you can turn Rules Checking off by selecting the toggle command **Turn Rules Checking On/Off**. You might want to do this while you perform an intermediate step that temporarily makes the tagging incorrect.

Viewing

While HoTMetaL provides a number of commands for controlling the presentation of text, including the ability to set font families, point sizes, and spacing, it's not the same as previewing in Mosaic. These settings bear no relationship to the way Mosaic will present the document. To make the previewing more useful, HoTMetaL has a **Preview** command, which launches Mosaic and loads the document.

There are two windows, launched from the **View** menu, that help in checking the construction of your document. **Show Structure View** (shown in Figure 7-14) brings up a window that shows the hierarchy of the entire document. Each line represents a new element and has a start tag, an end tag, and the text between them. The lines are indented to show the nesting of tags. For a close-up look at the structure of the selected element, use **Show Link and Context View**. When the selected element is nested within other elements, this window will show the hierarchical sequence up to the selected element. It doesn't show tags before or after the current hierarchy.

While you're still not an HTML expert, you're well on your way now. We haven't covered every single thing you can do with HTML, but you know enough now to create pages as sophisticated as most of what you see on the Web. For information on more advanced elements, see Appendix B.

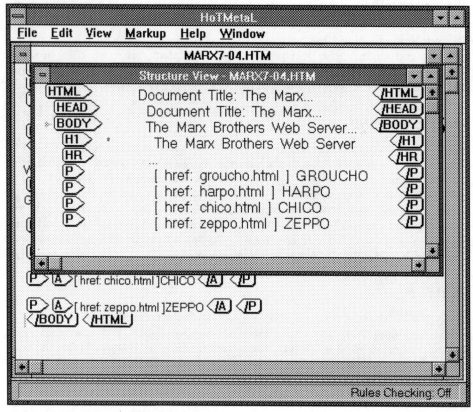

Figure 7–14. HoTMetaL's structure view

Resources

A Beginners Guide to HTML
http://www.ncsa.uiuc.edu/General/Internet/WWW/HTMLPrimer.html

A Beginners Guide to URLs
http://www.ncsa.uiuc.edu/demoweb/url-primer.html

HTML Quick Reference
http://kuhttp.cc.ukans.edu/lynx_help/HTML_quick.html

Hyper Text Markup Language (HTML)
http://info.cern.ch/hypertext/WWW/MarkUp/MarkUp.html

Style Guide
http://info.cern.ch/hypertext/WWW/Provider/Style/Overview.html

WWW Names and Addresses
http://info.cern.ch/hypertext/WWW/Addressing/Addressing.html

World Wide Web Initiative
http://info.cern.ch/hypertext/WWW/TheProject.html

ISO Latin Characters
http//info.cern.ch/hypertext/WWW/MarkUp/ISOlat1.html

CHAPTER EIGHT

FUTURE DIRECTIONS

W3O
WWW Project Information
VRML: Visualizing Web Space

The Mosaic interface and the World Wide Web information architecture will continue to evolve in new directions. In this chapter, we try to indicate what some of those directions might be and to describe how you can join in the discussions on the Net where the new developments are happening.

We begin with a story from *GNN NetNews* on W3O, the organization created by the Massachusetts Institute of Technology (MIT) and the European Laboratory for Particle Physics (CERN) to shape the future of the WWW. We also include a *GNN* interview by D.C. Denison with Professor Michael Dertouzos of MIT, a key player in creating this international organization. He talks about the goal of creating a Web that includes online entertainment, commerce, and education, and what needs to be done to make this happen.

Also in this chapter, we catalog the newsgroups, mailing lists, and Web servers where you can follow the most recent developments, such as the Virtual Reality Markup Language.

W3O

Almost from the beginning of the World Wide Web initiative at CERN, project leader Tim Berners-Lee recognized the need for a separate organization that could help to develop WWW standards, as well as much of the common code base. In the summer of 1994 that organization finally emerged, and it was named W3O. The organizing sponsors of W3O consortium are MIT and CERN. Berners-Lee will move from CERN to MIT to serve as the director of W3O.

At MIT, the Web initiative will be based at the Laboratory for Computer Science. Professor Michael L. Dertouzos is the director of the Lab. Dertouzos said that W3O aspires to "enhance the Web by developing the 'bulldozers and backhoes' of the information age, that will work for us—not the other way around, as is often the case today.

"We envision an information market where information and information services can be purchased, sold, or exchanged freely so as to improve the economic well-being and the quality of life of people throughout the world, and as a medium for education and the nurturing and integrating of different cultures."

W3O is expected to receive the enthusiastic support of the European Union. "It is of the utmost importance that these computer frameworks be worldwide frameworks," said Dr. Martin Bangemann, the Commissioner of the European Union in charge of industrial policy, information technologies and industries, and telecommunications. "The European Union intends to support this cooperative activity as an important step toward the Global Information Society," he said.

Dr. George Metakides, director of the European Strategic Program for Research and Development in Information Technologies (ESPRIT), which reports to Dr. Bangemann, commented, "Common information navigation tools will be essential for the development of the Global Information Infrastructure. This development of the World Wide Web provides a concrete example that will help us to understand better the transition to the information society."

At the time of the W3O announcement, Tim Berners-Lee commented, "The Web was conceived as a representation of mankind's knowledge, society, and commerce." It is becoming more secure, more interactive, and developing greater richness of meaning. An international base seemed essential to support its very rapid growth and its evolution, while also ensuring its stability.

"Throughout the world, information and communications technologies are generating a new industrial revolution already as significant and far-reaching as those of the past," according to the European Union's Bangemann. "A global information society is emerging which changes the way we work together and the way we live together. The engine driving the transition to the information society is the information infrastructure, which enables us to process, retrieve, and communicate information in whatever form it may take—oral, written, or visual—unconstrained by distance, time or volume."

As you might expect, you can follow the developments at W3O online. As of this writing, there are only a few pages on the Web about W3O, but that should change quickly.

The following URL will get you to the W3O server. (This server may be relocated to MIT.)

```
http://info.cern.ch/hypertext/WWW/Organization/Consortium/W3OSignature.html
```

MIT's Michael L. Dertouzos on W3O

To get a better sense of what W3O might do, as well as what interesting directions the Web might move in, we have an interview with MIT's Professor Dertouzos. This interview was conducted by D.C. Denison and originally appeared in *GNN NetNews* in August of 1994, several weeks after the formation of W3O had been announced.

A secretary gives the visiting reporter a simple way to know when Michael L. Dertouzos has arrived at MIT's Laboratory for Computer Science.

"He's the biggest man who will walk through the door," she says, pointing to the main entrance.

Sure enough, Dertouzos, the director of the Lab and a professor of computer science and electrical engineering at MIT, is easy to spot. Tall and courtly, he sweeps into the office, gathers up a couple of mugs of coffee and some fresh faxes (from Vice President Albert Gore's office, it turns out), and settles down to discuss some big ideas. Like Dertouzos' idea of an "information marketplace," which he has been promoting for 15 years, and the W3O, the brand new international initiative to develop and standardize the World Wide Web.

How did you get interested in the World Wide Web?

I was looking for a mechanism that would allow this Lab to concentrate its future research on the architecture of the global information infrastructure, with the emphasis on global. Second, I wanted something that already had millions of users, so it had the voice of reality, but was bendable. Then reality would bend us back, if we proposed stupid things, and we would bend it back, if we proposed clever or useful things.

I really want this lab to be an architect of tomorrow's information infrastructure. There are going to be so many people out there doing interfaces: Time/Warner will have a movie interface and a news interface; Bill Gates will have his own Microsoft interface, so that if you're in Excel you can hook up with somebody on the other side of the ocean who is also using Excel; the telcos will have an interface, each with its own look and feel; the publishers, the Murdochs, will have their own spin on an interface. Everyone wants to control that, because they see it as a very lucrative market. So there will be no shortage of me-toos, trying to plug you into the infrastructure. But no one's worried about the damn architecture. So I saw this as a fertile ground, for this Laboratory to focus on the architecture. And when I talk about architecture, I'm talking about how machines in one location will understand what the machines in another location want to do. Today, if you look at the Internet, they don't. It's human beings who have to understand. In fact the Web is human browsable.

Is there a better way, in your opinion?

Back in the industrial era, we invented machines, and they replaced our muscles. That was a simple thing to understand. We've also come up with ways to produce food by using only three percent of the population, instead of 50 percent. So what are we replacing in the information revolution? What would you say?

The work of finding and accessing information. The "legwork" it takes to locate sources of information. How's that?

The mundane mind work, if I may generalize from your words. You want to replace some of the mundane mind work. So in this lab, we're trying to work out schemes that will act as bulldozers and backhoes for the mind. That's a nice metaphor. The Web doesn't have bulldozers or backhoes; it has shovels. It welcomes you with lots of shovels that you have to operate. All it is now is a Web that links home pages and other pages all over the world: you click, you cross the ocean or the street, and then your brain has to go to work: you have to figure out, "What do I want to do?" and "What do I have to do?" It's like electronic mail: it does some wonderful things, but it has some terrible disadvantages.

What are its disadvantages?

It's another shovel in your hands. I can click my little finger and create a hundred copies of your message to me, and my response to you, and 100 minds have to at least read the message address to figure out what I'm telling them. Again, it's the human brain being overloaded. It is not evolution, in productivity terms, when you overload an ancient human brain. It's as if the Industrial Revolution came and you started telling people, "Now if you only start working harder with your muscles, we can offer you a lot of utopias." That's bull. It doesn't work. So viewed from that perspective, the current existing networks are nowhere near where we envision them. This is the vision that I have.

So you want to make things simpler.

Correct. But not only simpler. I see it as the human quest to increase productivity, to have others do his work. Technology is there to serve us.

What are the first things we can expect to see on future versions of the World Wide Web?

Recreation. There are 80 million households in the country, and a little over two TV sets in each household. That's more than 150 million TV sets. There are only 30 or 40 million PCs. There is also a well-known, $14 billion market that views videos. So the first application is clearly that one.

Do you think the Web can deliver that kind of entertainment?

Not in its current form. But the Web, suitably modified, could. But we're talking about the infrastructure of the future here, and that infrastructure clearly has to have the architecture to support recreation. So the first things you're going to see will probably be recreation. The Web today goes through slower lines, but there's nothing prohibiting people from running the Web through television's coaxial cable.

And after recreation?

After recreation, I see shopping and mail-order coming right away, because that's natural, once people get used to browsing. Another thrust will come from the business sector, and commerce, by which I mean the whole set of transactions that start with looking for things, move on to negotiations, move on to contracting, and move on to delivery and post delivery. All these steps can be very important, depending on what you're buying or selling. Then there's education, which is the toughest, because although there's plenty of talk about education, there isn't much money. Whereas with entertainment and commerce, there's money and perceived need. So the possibilities for education are beautiful, but will it really happen? The whole area of travel will also be big. But the initial thrust will probably be recreation and commerce. Then I see health care coming in big. There's money there, and the Web can help save both time and money. Financial services and group-work are other areas that show promise.

This seems to be a long way from the current system.

Things always look that way. If you ask people what they want, they generally want 20 percent more than they have—a few more features, smoother operation, etc. But we want to go 150 percent ahead.

How many people will be working on W3O?

I don't differentiate between W3O and the rest of the Lab. We have about 500 people working here, and about half of them will be working on the information infrastructure. But specific W3O people, working on the standard, and issuing new versions—probably around 12.

Is part of W3's appeal its scalability?

W3 is very clean and unmolested by too many fixed ideas, so you can put some things on it. And it can expand. But our own idea, since day one, has been to build this information market. We're interested in a market, not a utility where someone has all the knowledge and sells it. We're not interested in any of these dictatorial models; we want a market where buyers and sellers come together and buy and sell information. It's decentralized.

That's not what many corporations are building now.

No, this is not what's happening today. The scenarios you see today will make it possible for you to watch a movie, but if you want to then sell a service, you won't be able to. So we don't have a market. We don't have an equal place where you and I can transact. We have a broadcast medium, and that's what everybody's after: control, which means broadcast. Never mind if they give you some interaction back, so you can choose what you can buy, it's still broadcast. I've given a name to these models: I call them spiders, because they have a hub, and there's one way out, and they don't let you come back in. There are all sorts of spiders. The European telephone company is a spider: they think that they are going to offer every service you're going to need. That's another spider that prohibits an information market.

If you stop and think about it, it's not in the interest of any single capitalistic agency to promote a universal infrastructure. Any more than it's in the interest of any capitalistic agency to promote a highway system for cars. Who built the highway system in this country? The government. I'm not a socialist, I'm a capitalist, but there are some things that the government has to stimulate. This is one of them. People left to their own devices are going to build spiders, and it will take us 20 years before people will realize, which they will, that there's more money in converting spiders to highways. But by then there may be a lot of things already frozen in place.

How will you head off all these spider-builders?

That's why we're the architects. That's one of our noble duties—to say to people, "Yes, guys, these spiders are great for sending movies to the home, and it's even great to sell L.L. Bean products. But you won't be able to buy, from that home-dweller, his ability to retouch photographs. You won't be able to buy, from that homedweller, his or her ability to work on insurance forms. The way you're going, all you'll be able to get from that homedweller are clicks that are going to say, 'Buy this, sell that, do this, do that.' He cannot put any of his own stuff on. That's fine. We'll offer you an architecture where you can do all that. But our architecture has hooks. So later, when you see the light, and you see that there's some revenue there, we can turn on that hook, and that person can sell." And that person can get on the highway system.

Did you see W3 as a place where a market structure was already working, on a small scale?

W3 already has a great deal of this information market idea in it. It's got two beautiful things. The first is an obvious one, that anyone can produce something. You can create a home page that's as elaborate or as silly as you want. The second part of this is that there are 30 million of you doing this, and it is growing into a beautiful edifice. That's how it will continue to grow: if you do a great Web demo for a health center, then every health center and clinic is going to want to be Webbed. That's how it will work.

It's already working like that.

Yes, but what we have now is a chaotic evolution of servers with no order. The Internet, really, has no order. It's a mud field, and every ten kilometers of mud, you find a little diamond. That's a situation we will be working to improve.

What were the negotiations like, with CERN, when you were trying to put W3O together?

The elements of the deal are really quite obvious. Tim Berners-Lee invented the Web, at CERN, and they have a great understanding of the Web, and a great community of people using the Web. On our part, at MIT, we have the experience with the X Consortium, and our systems work for the last 30 years. And we have architectural research in progress, on the information infrastructure, that is second to none worldwide.

What's going to attract corporations to the W3O Consortium?

Corporations are not stupid. They don't want to miss the next standard. So you offer them a reasonable entry, financially and otherwise, into a consortium, as we did with the X Consortium. You make sure they don't have any spider controls, but you be sure to listen to them, so that they evolve the standard with what they want to see changed, without constraining others from using it. If you get the right balance between openness and response to your users—that is one of the most accepted methods of evolving a standard. It's much faster than an international committee.

Why?

Because you have a standard czar, in this case Tim Berners-Lee, who will be in charge of the consortium. And you have a team of elders, 12 people who will constitute his council. At least half of them will come from the consortium; the other half will be knowledgeable technologists and others whom he will consult. All year long people will be saying, "Gee, Tim, wouldn't it be nice if we had X or Y or Z in there?" Or they're saying, "Tim, that thing that you put in last year—that's a piece of junk." Or they're saying, "That feature you put in, that's fantastic." So he listens to all this, he talks to his elders, then come January 1 he drops the sword and he says, "The next version, number 9, of the W3 standard is this." And the minute he issues that, everybody—and I mean everybody—says "Thank God, we have one place where these decisions are made." That honeymoon lasts precisely one day. The very next day they're back bitching and saying, "Let's make this change, that change . . . " That's how the standard works.

So any company that knows about this process—and they all do—is going to say to themselves, "Hey look, there are some pretty good people at W3O, like the inventor, and CERN, and MIT. Maybe there's just a chance that they're going to do something. Can I afford not to be there?" And we need these people. Because without the manufacturers, who are going to build this stuff, and without the users, and without the technologists, who we represent, we don't have anything. You've got to have all three components: users, makers, and researchers.

How much of a role are you going to play?

This subject happens to be a rather serious interest of mine, the information infrastructure. I'm writing a book on it. So I'll stop in and ask questions, but I'm not going to interfere. This is really better left to other people. But I'll be watching, making sure that we carve a path that is going to open the usage of these things to the world, and create an infrastructure, rather than create a spider.

How will you roll out advances to WWW?

By a system of what I call protocol grafts. You know the way you graft a branch on a tree and it either takes or it doesn't? We are going to be declaring, in a given standard version, that "Here is the standard, and here is the graft region that has the six new things in it. They are not part of the standard; they are for people who want to play. But please send your comments." In the next version, based on the comments, two of these six grafts might make it into the standard, three might drop off, and one might stay for another year of observation. And three new grafts might be added. That's how I plan to resolve these tensions in an orderly way. Otherwise, the Web is going to remain a human-browsable network, which is not very useful. And my people's great ideas will remain unsorted, as to which ones are bull or great.

What would be an example of a graft?

Let's say an automated vocabulary, with 100 nouns and 100 verbs, which every server on the Web that implements that standard can now understand. The verbs could be of the form, "Have you?" or be declarative, of the form, "I sent you," or "I ask you to send me" or "I ask, do you have?" or "Can you show me how?" And there may be one hundred nouns, having to do with "a file named __" or "a picture named __" or statements of the form "I don't understand." So maybe we announce, "We're putting in this graft extension, a little language that augments the Web, and if you install this software, then you'll be able to not only finger-click, but do some things automatically." So we'll try it as a graft. Nobody is compelled to use it. In fact, if you want simplicity, ask for the version without this. Then, whenever somebody hits you with it, they will get back the message, "Sorry, this node does not understand graft #16." But people being as adventurous as they are, they'll go for the grafts.

The Internet doesn't lack for adventurous people.

That's right. You have 15 million adventurous people. Even if half of them say "screw it," that still leaves enough for me to know if a given graft will take or not. And I'm not just talking about the techies. I want to get the regular human beings. So look for deals with some of the entertainment companies.

When will we see the first new version of WWW coming out of W3O?

I expect nothing before a year and a half. Tim Berners-Lee will start in September (1994). If we assume version 1.0 was what happened in Geneva, the very earliest you can expect to see version 2.0 will be January '96. Maybe.

WWW Project Information

The largest repository of the information about the WWW is online, and organized at CERN. The URL for the WWW Project is:

```
http://info.cern.ch/hypertext/WWW/TheProject.html
```

You will find various lists of resources, as well as pointers to technical information about the Web. We have summarized the key information resources below.

WWW Newsgroups

If you're interested in following, or taking part in, the development of the Web, you can participate in several newsgroups. Here is a list of Web-related newsgroups.

comp.infosystems.www.users

This newsgroup is the best starting place for learning about using the Web. It is a forum for the discussion of Web browsers and their use with various Internet information sources. Among the topics covered in this group: new user questions, client setup questions, client bug reports, questions on how to locate information on the Web, and comparisons between various client packages.

comp.infosystems.www.providers

This newsgroup is a forum for the discussion of Web server software and presenting information to users. Topics covered include: general server design, setup questions, server bug reports, security issues, HTML page design, and other concerns of information providers.

comp.infosystems.www.misc

A forum for general discussion of Web-related topics that are not covered by the other newsgroups in the hierarchy. According to CERN, "This will likely include discussions of the Web's future, politicking regarding changes in the structure and protocols of the Web that affect both clients and servers, etc."

Mailing Lists

To join any of the CERN mailing lists, send email to *listserv@info.cern.ch* with the following message:

```
subscribe list-name your-name
```

in the body of the message. For example:

```
subscribe www-announce "Dale Dougherty"
```

If you need more information about CERN's mailing lists, use the following URL:

```
http://info.cern.ch/hypertext/WWW/Administration/Mailing/Overview.html
```

The CERN mailing lists are described in the sections that follow. Many are available in archive form. If the archive is organized by a program called **Hypermail**, the messages can be viewed sorted by date, subject, or author.

www-announce

A mailing list for anyone interested in WWW, its progress, new data sources, or new software releases. There is also an archive of the list, which is accessible through Mosaic. The URL for the archive is:

```
http://info.cern.ch/hypertext/WWW/Archive/www-announce
```

www-html

Technical discussions of HTML and HTMLPlus. This is a technical mailing list consisting of design discussions only. This is not the place to ask basic questions about writing HTML, but if you're interested in following the nitty-gritty of the HTML language, you may want to subscribe to this list.

There is also a hypertext-based archive for this mailing list at:

```
http://info.cern.ch/hypertext/WWW/Archive/www-html
```

www-proxy

This mailing list is for a technical discussion about WWW proxies, caching, and future directions.

www-talk

Technical discussion for those developing WWW software or with a deep interest in WWW. (Please keep this to WWW technical design only, *not* general questions from non-developers.) See the hypertext archive at:

```
http://gummo.stanford.edu/html/hypermail/archives.html
```

VRML: Visualizing Web Space

The idea behind the Virtual Reality Markup Language (VRML) is to create a non-proprietary, platform-independent language, much like HTML, that would allow authors to create virtual reality "scenes." Users of virtual reality servers would be able to walk around a space and push open doors to other parts of the Web. While, as of this writing, VRML is still very much in the "talking about" phase, there is a working specification for VRML, developed by Mark Pesce and Anthony Parisi of the Labyrinth Group in San Francisco.

VRML Resources

The VRML Web site contains papers, specifications, and links to other VR-related projects. The URL is:

```
http://www.wired.com/vrml/
```

You can subscribe to the www-vrml mailing list by sending email to:

```
majordomo@wired.com
```

with the following in the body of the message:

```
subscribe www-vrml your-email-address
```

MOSAIC REFERENCE GUIDE

The Toolbar
The Menus

While using Mosaic is a fairly intuitive experience, the program includes several features that are quite helpful in managing your Mosaic session. This appendix provides a comprehensive guide to Mosaic's toolbar and menu commands. The interface is described in Chapter 2, *Getting Started with Mosaic.*

The Toolbar

The toolbar contains icons and displays information that helps you understand where you are and how to get to your next destination.

Back and Forward Arrows

On the left side of the toolbar is the **Back** arrow, which points to the left. You use this button to display the page you were last viewing. Next to it, pointing to the right, is the **Forward** arrow. It works the same way, only in reverse. Normally the **Forward** arrow is dimmed; if you use the **Back** arrow, the **Forward** arrow becomes active, allowing you to return to your most recently downloaded page.

It's kind of like adding pages to a book. Every time you download a new page, you are adding that page to the back of your book; that page then becomes the last page of the book. Flipping back brings you to pages that were downloaded earlier; flipping forward takes you to pages added later.

This navigation process works well for moving through documents held in the cache. It gets a bit confusing, however, if you move too far back. When you move to a document that is not in the cache, Mosaic will download that document; that file will then become the most recent document. The solution is to use **Back** and **Forward** only to move in small increments; use **History** or **Hotlist** to take larger steps.

URL Display

On the left side of the toolbar, you will see a field labeled **URL**. This field tells you the URL of your current document. For instance, when you're looking at the *GNN Home* page, this field reads *http://gnn.com/GNNhome.html*. This text can be copied to the clipboard with the CTRL-C command, just like any other text. This is a handy feature if you want to email a URL to your friends or just keep a list of favorite URLs handy.

The Menus

There are five menus in Mosaic: **File**, **Edit**, **Navigate**, **Windows**, and **Help**. These menus lets you manage files, change display characteristics, navigate the Web, manage windows, and display online help.

The File Menu

The **File** menu has commands for file management operations like opening, saving, closing, and printing files.

New Window

Mosaic lets you open numerous windows, so you can keep many different documents open on your screen at the same time. This can save quite a bit of time in going back and forth to your most frequently used documents. For instance, you could keep *GNN* open in one window and explore other Web offerings in another window. Then, instead of having to find your way back to *GNN*, just switch to the *GNN* window.

Open URL

As described in Chapter 2, **Open URL** lets you enter a URL in a field. Mosaic will then contact the server and get the file for you. Because you have to enter the whole string by hand, it's quite easy to make a mistake. If you get an error message, such as "The program couldn't find the document" or "The program couldn't find the server," check to make sure you entered the URL correctly. Some directories and filenames are case-sensitive, so make sure you entered the URL exactly.

Open Local

When you're writing HTML documents, it's quite helpful to preview them in Mosaic. To view HTML documents on your PC, use the **Open Local** command. It opens a standard Windows dialog box showing disks and directories. **Open Local** is handy when writing HTML documents because mistakes are sometimes hard to catch when looking at ASCII text, but they become glaringly obvious when displayed in Mosaic. Remember, you must give your HTML documents a name with the extension *.htm*. If you don't, Mosaic will display the file as plain text. You can also use **Open Local** to view non-HTML files on your hard disk.

Save As

This command lets you save the current document to your hard disk as either an HTML document or as plain text with the HTML codes stripped out. This comes in handy if there's a long, particularly useful document that you want to read offline. Just save it as HTML and use the **Open Local** command to view it in Mosaic. Saving as text is better if you plan to put the document in a document of your own, for instance, a memo that you create in a word processing or page layout program.

Close and Close All

These are used to close windows. **Close** only closes the active window, while **Close All** closes all open windows.

Print

Selecting the **Print** option prints all pages in the current document. When you print from Mosaic, it prints the document with the margins and header and footer information specified in the **Page Setup** dialog.

Page Setup

Page Setup lets you set the margins and header and footer information for printing the current document. The default margins are .75 -inch on all sides. The headers are set to display the document title in the upper left, the page number in the upper right, the date in the lower left, and the time in the lower right.

Print Setup

Selecting this option opens the *Print* dialog box, where you can specify your printer, the printing range (either "all" or a range from a starting page to an ending page), and the number of copies. There is also a checkbox to collate when printing multiple copies. Clicking **OK** prints the pages you requested.

Beneath the **OK** and **Cancel** buttons is a button labeled **Setup**. Clicking this button takes you to the Print Setup dialog, where you can specify a printer, paper size, and page orientation (portrait or landscape). Clicking **OK** here takes you back to the **Print** dialog.

Exit

Exit quits the program.

Edit menu

The **Edit** menu contains commands that deal with the text of a document.

Cut, Copy, and Paste

Unlike with other Windows programs, you can't cut, copy, or paste text displayed in Mosaic. That's because the document displayed in Mosaic is really just a representation of the actual HTML file. These commands do have a useful function in Mosaic, however; you can select and copy the text in the toolbar's URL field and paste that into a word processing document or email message. The **Open URL** command also works with cut, copy, and paste operations.

Find and Find Again

The **Find** command lets you search the current document for a text string, which is highlighted in the document when found. The dialog box includes two checkboxes, one for matching case and one for starting from the top of the document. **Find Again** repeats the search without opening the **Find** dialog box. **Find Again** saves you the step of having to click **OK** within the dialog box.

View Source

This command lets you see the HTML version of the document. It's useful for people who are previewing their HTML documents in Mosaic or who want to see how somebody else achieved a certain result. You cannot select, copy, cut, or paste from the **View Source** window, however; you can only view and save.

Preferences

The **Preferences** dialog box lets you control certain aspects of the way Mosaic displays documents to you. **Preferences** is discussed in more detail in Chapter 5, *Customizing Mosaic*.

Load Images Automatically
Checking this option sets Mosaic to download inline graphics when downloading an HTML document. Unchecking it downloads only the HTML page, with images replaced by generic picture icons or alternative text, if specified.

Underline Links
When this option is checked, Mosaic underlines links.

Set Home Page
You can change your home page by entering a URL in this field.

Proxy Server
If your organization uses a proxy server, you need to specify the server name in this field.

Style Sheets

You can change the way Mosaic formats documents by selecting a different style sheet from this pop-up menu.

Navigate Menu

The Navigate menu contains the options that you will use most often as you traverse the Web.

Back and Forward

These menu items correspond to the **Back** and **Forward** buttons on the toolbar.

History

The **History** window contains a list of all the documents you have visited since you first ran the program; it doesn't clear when you quit the program. **History** also contains several buttons that let you manage the list.

Delete

To delete entries from the **History** list, select a document title and click **Delete**. Mosaic doesn't ask you to confirm the action.

Edit

Selecting a document title and clicking on **Edit** opens a window that lets you change the title and URL of the document.

Scan Current

Scan Current extracts all of the links in your current page and adds them to the list.

Go To

Go To is the equivalent of **OK** in Windows dialog boxes. Selecting a document title and clicking **Go To** downloads that document.

Close

Close exits the **History** window.

Hotlist

When you find servers you want to be able to get to quickly, you can add them to your hotlist. The **Hotlist** window has several commands for managing your hotlist.

Add Current

Clicking on this button adds the current document to your hotlist. When you add Web documents, their titles are displayed in the list. When you add non-Web documents, their URLs are displayed.

Delete

To delete a document from your hotlist, select the document title and click on the **Delete** button.

Edit

To change the document title displayed in the hotlist, select the title and click on **Edit**. This brings up a window that lets you change the title and URL of the selected document. This is especially handy for non-Web documents, for which Mosaic displays URLs as titles. You may want to change the URLs of documents that have changed location, but it's safer to go to the new location, add that document to your hotlist, and then delete the old one.

Scan Current

Scan Current extracts all the URLs of the current document and adds them to your hotlist.

Export

Export creates an HTML document consisting of all of the document titles and URLs in your hotlist. Each title in the document is an active link. When you click on **Export**, Mosaic asks you to name the document, which it then creates and immediately displays.

Go To

Selecting a title and clicking on **Go To** downloads the selected document.

Close

Close closes the **Hotlist** window.

Add Current to Hotlist

This option adds the current document to your hotlist, the same as the **Add Current** button in the **Hotlist** window.

Load Missing Images

If you set Mosaic not to automatically download inline graphics, it will draw generic picture icons where the pictures would be. If you want to see all the images on the page, however, just choose the **Load Missing Images** command and Mosaic will download them for you.

Reload

This command simply downloads the same page over again. It is useful when Mosaic has a problem displaying an image on your screen. It is often used when writing HTML documents and previewing them in Mosaic. When you edit an HTML document, you can just choose **Reload** to preview the new version.

Windows

The **Windows** menu lists all of your open windows. You can switch windows by selecting the appropriate document title from the window. This menu also contains two commands to organize windows—**Tile** and **Cascade**. **Tile** redraws your screen so each window takes up the same amount of space. **Cascade** arranges open windows so that the title bar of each window is visible.

GNN

The **GNN** menu lets you move directly to several centers and special-interest publications in *GNN*.

Help

Mosaic comes with an online help file that explains the interface and the menu operations.

HTML REFERENCE GUIDE

Table B-1: Tags

Tag	End Tag	Description
<HTML>	</HTML>	Starts/ends document
<HEAD>	</HEAD>	Starts/ends header
<TITLE>	</TITLE>	Starts/ends title
<BODY>	</BODY>	Starts/ends body
<H1>,<H2>, etc.	</H1>,</H2>, etc.	Starts/ends heading text
<P>	N/A	Starts new paragraph
 	N/A	Inserts line break
<HR>	N/A	Inserts horizontal rule
<EM>	</EM>	Surrounds emphasized text
<STRONG>	</STRONG>	Surrounds stronger text
<B>	</B>	Surrounds bold text
<I>	</I>	Surrounds italic text
<U>	</U>	Surrounds underlined text
<ADDRESS>	</ADDRESS>	Surrounds text in address format
<BLOCKQUOTE>	</BLOCKQUOTE>	Surrounds text in blockquote format
<PRE>	</PRE>	Surrounds preformatted text
<DL>	</DL>	Starts/ends glossary
<DT>	N/A	Precedes term entry in glossary
<DD>	N/A	Precedes term definition in glossary
<UL>	</UL>	Starts/ends unordered list
<OL>	</OL>	Starts/ends ordered list
<LI>	N/A	Precedes entries in list
<A>	</A>	Surrounds anchor; start tag requires attributes
<IMG>	N/A	Inserts inline graphic

Table B-2: Tag Attributes

Tag	End Tag	Attribute	Description	Values
<A>	</A>			
		HREF	Defines link destination	File name or anchor name
		NAME	Gives symbolic name to anchor	Any one-word name
<IMG>	N/A			
		SOURCE	Defines image source file	File name
		ALIGN	Specifies alignment	TOP, MIDDLE, BOTTOM
		ALT	Specifies alternate text	Any text

GLOSSARY

access provider

See "Internet Service Provider."

anchor

The location of a hypertext link in a document; it can be used to describe the link as it appears in text or graphics as well as the place that the link references.

Archie

A program used to locate files that are publicly available by anonymous FTP.

ARPAnet

An experimental network established in the 1970's that served as a test environment for the software on which the Internet is based. No longer in existence.

attributes

(a) SGML (and HTML) tags may accept attributes that further define their usage, much as parameters are used with command-line options. A tag may be followed by an attribute, which in turn is assigned a particular value.

(b) Configurable characteristics of Mosaic that determine how the program functions and how it displays elements on your screen.

baud

When transmitting data, the number of times the medium's "state" changes per second. For example: a 14.4K baud modem changes the signal it sends on the phone line 14,400 times per second. Since each change in state can correspond to multiple bits of data, the actual bit rate of data transfer may exceed the baud rate. See also "bits per second."

bits per second (bps)

The speed at which bits are transmitted over a communication medium.

browser

A program that interprets and displays HTML documents.

cache

Generically speaking, a location in memory where data is stored for easy retrieval, or the process of storing them. Some versions of Mosaic cache the document previously viewed so you can return to it easily. You can configure

Mosaic to hold an additional number of documents and images in the cache. If a document or image is not available in the cache, Mosaic has to return to the Internet to retrieve it.

CERN

The European Particle Physics Laboratory (CERN) in Geneva, Switzerland; hypertext technologies developed at CERN to allow physicists to share information provided the basis for the World Wide Web.

client

A software application that works on your behalf to extract some service from a server somewhere on the network.

dialup

(a) To connect to a computer by calling it up on the telephone. Often, "dialup" only refers to the kind of connection you make when using a terminal emulator and a regular modem. For the technoids: switched character-oriented asynchronous communication.

(b) A port that accepts dialup connections. ("How many dialup ports on your computer?")

dialup account

A type of Internet connection that operates over standard phone lines. Dialup accounts are of two types: shell accounts and PPP/SLIP accounts.

To use a shell account, you typically use a telecommunications program to dial the Internet host and log in. This is a cheap and easy method, but has many limitations; for example, you can't use Mosaic.

A PPP/SLIP account, which requires a high-speed modem, actually puts your computer on the network and allows you to use Mosaic.

See also "Mosaic," "shell," "PPP," "SLIP," and "dedicated line."

download

To transfer data from a remote server to your local system. The FTP program is often used to download files.

DNS

The Domain Name System; a distributed database system for translating computer names (like **ruby.ora.com**) into numeric Internet addresses (like 194.56.78.2), and vice-versa. DNS allows you to use the Internet without remembering long lists of numbers.

dedicated line

A permanently connected private telephone line between two locations. Dedicated lines are typically used to connect a moderate-sized local network to an Internet service provider. If your Internet connection is provided by a dedicated line, you should be able to use Mosaic. See also "Mosaic" and "dialup account."

Ethernet

A kind of "local area network" (or LAN). It's difficult to define an Ethernet because there are several different kinds of wiring, which support different communication speeds, ranging from 2 to 10 million bits per second. What makes an Ethernet an Ethernet is the way the computers on the network decide whose turn it is to talk. Computers using TCP/IP are frequently connected to the Internet over an Ethernet. (Say that three times fast.)

FAQ

An acronym that generally refers to a list of frequently asked questions and their answers, or a question from the list. Many USENET newsgroups and some non-USENET mailing lists maintain FAQ lists (FAQs) so that participants don't spend a lot of time answering the same set of questions.

firewall

See "security firewall."

FTP

(a) The File Transfer Protocol; a protocol that defines how to transfer files from one computer to another.

(b) An application program that moves files using the File Transfer Protocol.

gateway

A computer system that transfers data between normally incompatible applications or networks. It reformats the data so that it is acceptable for the new network (or application) before passing it on. A gateway may connect two dissimilar networks, like DECnet and the Internet; or it might allow two incompatible applications to communicate over the same network (like mail systems with different message formats).

GIF

GIF refers to the Graphics Interchange Format, a graphics file format developed by CompuServe, Inc., which is used on a variety of platforms and systems. GIF is one of the most widely used formats for storing complex graphics, and one of only two formats in which inline images can appear in an HTML document. See also "XBM."

Gopher

A menu-based system for exploring Internet resources; the items are arranged in a hierarchy and each item represents either a file or a directory.

History

A function of the Mosaic browser that keeps track of all the documents you visit and allows you to call them up again.

home page

(a) The graphical door to the information a server provides. The home page is generally a screen or window full of information in which links to related information are included.

(b) A document that you specify for Mosaic to display when you launch the program and that acts as a "safe port" as you navigate the Web.

host

> (a) Generically, a computer.
>
> (b) Sometimes, a computer that provides resources to the Internet; also called an Internet host computer.

Hotlist

> A function of the Mosaic browser that allows you to keep a list of the documents you're most interested in and to call them up again.

HoTMetaL

> A program from SoftQuad that assists you in formatting documents using HTML codes; available both as freeware and as a commercial product.

HTML

> The HyperText Markup Language, a subset of SGML, provides codes used to format hypertext documents. Individual codes are used to define the hierarchy and nature of the various components of the document, as well as to specify hypertext links.

HTTP

> The HyperText Transfer Protocol, a fixed set of messages and replies whereby a client and server communicate during a hypertext link.

hyperlink

> See "link."

hypermedia

> See "hypertext."

hypertext

> Any document that contains links to other documents; selecting a link automatically displays the second document.

IAB

> See the "Internet Architecture Board."

IETF

> See the "Internet Engineering Task Force."

ISP

> See "Internet Service Provider."

inline image

> An inline image is a graphic image that appears within the current hypertext page. See also "linked image."

Internet

> (a) Generally (not capitalized), any collection of distinct networks working together as one.
>
> (b) Specifically (capitalized), the world-wide "network of networks," which are connected to each other using the Internet protocol and other similar protocols. The Internet provides file transfer, remote login, electronic mail, news, and other services.

Internet Architecture Board (IAB)

The group that makes decisions about standards and other important issues.

Internet Engineering Task Force (IETF)

A volunteer group that investigates and solves technical problems and makes recommendations to the Internet Architecture Board (IAB).

Internet resources

Public information available via the Internet.

Internet Service Provider (ISP)

An organization that provides connections to a part of the Internet. If you want to connect your company's network, or even your personal computer, to the Internet, you have to talk to a "service provider."

ISO

The International Standards Organization (or International Organization for Standardization); an organization that has defined a different set of network protocols, called the ISO/OSI protocols. In theory, the ISO/OSI protocols will eventually replace the Internet protocols. When and if this will actually happen is a hotly debated topic.

JPEG

JPEG (pronounced "jay-peg"), which is an acronym for the Joint Photographic Experts Group, refers to a standards committee, a method of file compression, and a graphics file format. The committee originated from within the International Standards Organization (ISO) to research and develop standards for the transmission of image data over networks. The results were a highly successful method of data compression and several closely associated file formats to store the data. JPEG files typically contain photographs, video stills, or other complex images. Since Mosaic cannot display JPEG format files as "inline images," it launches a special viewer window in which the images are displayed.

LAN

See "Local Area Network."

leased line

See "dedicated line."

link

In hypertext documents, the connection from one document to another. See also "anchor."

linked image

A linked image is a graphic image that appears in a file separate from the current hypertext page; it is displayed by selecting a link. See also "inline image."

Local Area Network (LAN)

A grouping of computers that are physically connected within a fairly limited location.

Lynx

A character-based browsing program developed at the University of Kansas.

MIME

The Multipurpose Internet Mail Extensions protocol (MIME), that defines a number of content types and subtypes, which allow programs like Mosaic to recognize different kinds of files and deal with them appropriately. The MIME type specifies what kind of file it is, such as image, audio, or video, and the subtype gives the precise file format.

modem

A piece of equipment that connects a computer to a data transmission line (typically a telephone line). Most people use modems that transfer data at speeds ranging from 1200 bits per second (bps) to 19.2 Kbps. There are also modems providing higher speeds and supporting other media. These are used for special purposes—for example, to connect a large local network to its network provider over a leased line.

Mosaic

A graphical browser for the World Wide Web that supports hypermedia. Mosaic is often used incorrectly as a synonym for the World Wide Web.

MPEG

An acronym (pronounced "em-peg") for the Motion Picture Experts Group. MPEG denotes a standards committee, a method of file compression, and a graphics file format. The main application for MPEG is the storage of audio and video data on CD-ROMs for use in multimedia systems. Since Mosaic cannot display MPEG format files as inline images, it launches a special viewer window in which the images are displayed.

MUD/MOO

MUD refers to Multi-User Dungeon, a group of role-playing games modelled on the original "Dungeons and Dragons" games. MUDs have also been used as conferencing tools and educational aids. A MOO is an object-oriented MUD. Some experimental Web servers are set up with interactive MUD/MOO interfaces.

multimedia

Documents that include different kinds of data, for example, text, audio, and video.

NCSA

The National Center for Supercomputing Applications; NCSA produces a public domain version of the Mosaic browsing program and licenses the technology to developers.

NFS

The Network File System; a set of protocols that allows you to use files on other network machines as if they were local. So, rather than using FTP to transfer a file to your local computer, you can read it, write it, or edit it on the remote computer—using the same commands that you would use locally. NFS was originally developed by Sun Microsystems, Inc., and is widely used.

NSFNET

The National Science Foundation Network; the NSFNET is *not* the Internet. It's just one of the networks that make up the Internet.

OSI

Open Systems Interconnect; another set of network protocols. See "ISO."

packet

A bundle of data. On the Internet, data is broken up into small chunks, called "packets"; each packet traverses the network independently. Packet sizes can vary from roughly 40 to 32,000 bytes, depending on network hardware and media, but packets are normally less than 1500 bytes long.

port

(a) A number that identifies a particular Internet application. When your computer sends a packet to another computer, that packet contains information about what protocol it's using (e.g., TCP), and what application it's trying to communicate with. The "port number" identifies the application.

(b) One of a computer's physical input/output channels (i.e., a plug on the back).

Unfortunately, these two meanings are completely unrelated. The first is more common when you're talking about the Internet (as in "**telnet** to port 1000"); the second is more common when you're talking about hardware ("connect your modem to the serial port on the back of your computer").

PPP

Point-to-Point Protocol; a protocol that allows a computer to use the TCP/IP (Internet) protocols (and become a full-fledged Internet member) with a standard telephone line and a high-speed modem. Although PPP is less common than SLIP, it's quickly increasing in popularity.

PPP/SLIP account

See "dialup account."

protocol

Simply, a definition of how computers will act when talking to each other. Protocol definitions range from how bits are placed on a wire to the format of an electronic mail message. Standard protocols allow computers from different manufacturers to communicate; the computers can use completely different software, providing that the programs running on both ends agree on what the data means.

proxy server

A server on the Internet that provides indirect Internet access to systems excluded from a direct connection by a security firewall.

RFC

A Request For Comments; a set of papers in which the Internet's standards, proposed standards, and generally agreed-upon ideas are documented and published.

router

A system that transfers data between two networks that use the same protocols. The networks may differ in physical characteristics (e.g., a router may transfer data between an Ethernet and a leased telephone line).

security firewall

A system that isolates an organization's computers from external access, as through the Internet. The organization sometimes provides some Internet access through use of a proxy system. The firewall is intended to protect other machines at the site from potential tampering from the Net.

server

(a) Software that allows a computer to offer a service to another computer. Other computers contact the server program by means of matching client software.

(b) The computer on which the server software runs.

service provider

See "Internet Service Provider."

SGML

Standard Generalized Markup Language; a set of codes used to format documents. Individual codes are used to define the hierarchy and nature of the various components of a document; for example, as headers, options, variables, etc.

shell

On a UNIX system, software that accepts and processes command lines from your terminal. UNIX has multiple shells available (e.g., C shell, Bourne shell, Korn shell), each with slightly different command formats and facilities.

shell account

See "dialup account."

SLIP

Serial Line IP (Internet Protocol); a protocol that allows a computer to use the Internet protocols (and become a full-fledged Internet member) with a standard telephone line and a high-speed modem. SLIP is being superseded by PPP, but still in common use.

tags

In HTML, tags are the codes that determine both the structure of information within a document and its presentation.

TCP/IP

Transmission Control Protocol/Internet Protocol; the most important of the protocols on which the Internet is based. TCP is a reliable connection-oriented protocol; IP allows a packet to traverse multiple networks on the way to its final destination.

TELNET

(a) A "terminal emulation" protocol that allows you to log in to other computer systems on the Internet.

(b) An application program that allows you to log in to another computer system using the TELNET protocol.

TIFF

The Tag Image File Format, a graphics file format developed by Aldus Corporation, which has become a standard format found in most paint, imaging, and desktop publishing programs. TIFF is both powerful and flexible, and allows for storage of grayscale and color images.

URL

Uniform Resource Locator; the address of a document on the World Wide Web. The address is contained in a link, which a client interprets in order to connect with the proper server.

USENET

An informal, rather anarchic, group of systems that exchange "news." News is essentially similar to "bulletin boards" on other networks. USENET actually predates the Internet, but these days, the Internet is used to transfer much of the USENET's traffic.

Veronica

A service that allows you to search all Gopher sites for menu items (files, directories, and other resources).

viewer

A program Mosaic launches as needed to display a file in a format it cannot handle internally. For instance, Mosaic launches an MPEG player program to display an MPEG video file in a separate window because it cannot interpret this format.

visit

You access a World Wide Web document via a hypertext link. The anchor of a document that has been visited has a different appearance than the anchor of a link you haven't accessed.

W3O

An organization created by the Massachusetts Institute of Technology (MIT) and CERN to direct the development of the World Wide Web.

WAIS

See "Wide-Area Information Servers."

WAN

See "Wide Area Network."

Wide-Area Information Servers (WAIS)

A very powerful search-and-retrieval system for information in databases (or libraries) across the Internet. WAIS databases are gradually being adopted for general information storage and retrieval by the Internet community.

Wide Area Network (WAN)

A grouping of computers that are connected over communication lines, usually in a wide geographic area such as a state, country, or continent.

World Wide Web (WWW)

A hypertext-based system for finding and accessing Internet resources.

WWW

See "World Wide Web."

XBM

XBM refers to the X Bitmap graphics file format, which is the standard for bitmap image files in the X Window System. XBM files contain simple, two-tone images. XBM is one of only two formats in which inline images can appear in an HTML document. See also "GIF."

X Window System

A network-based windowing system, originally developed at the Massachusetts Institute of Technology (MIT); X is most frequently run in combination with the UNIX operating system.

INDEX

About the Authors

Dale Dougherty is manager of O'Reilly's Digital Media Group. He is publisher of the *Global Network Navigator*. He is also an editor and writer for O'Reilly & Associates. Among other books, Dale has written *sed & awk, UNIX Text Processing* (with Tim O'Reilly), *Using UUCP & Usenet* (with Grace Todino), and *Guide to the Pick System*.

Richard Koman is an editor for the *Global Network Navigator*. He is also technology editor for *Communication Arts*, a national graphic design magazine, and former editor of *Online Design*, a California monthly covering electronic design, graphics, and multimedia. He has covered design, publishing, and printing technology for a variety of publications.

Colophon

Our look is the result of reader comments, our own experimentation, and feedback from distribution channels.

Distinctive covers complement our distinctive approach to technical topics, breathing personality and life into potentially dry subjects.

The image featured on the cover of *The Mosaic Handbook for Microsoft Windows* is of a sailor on lookout in a crow's nest. It is likely that this particular crow's nest was attached to the mast of a late 19th century Arctic whaling vessel.

During the whaling industry's height, from about 1820 to the onset of the Civil War, more than 500 ships and 15,000 men, mostly from New England, were employed in the trade at any given time. These ships plied the Altantic, Pacific, and Indian oceans, hunting mainly sperm whales. The oil derived from the blubber of the sperm whale was considered to be the finest.

By the time the Civil War began, overharvesting had greatly depleted the whale population. New England's whaling fleet was diminished by the War, and the increased availability of petroleum led to a decreased need for the oil of the sperm whale. Whalers shifted their focus to Arctic Ocean, and the huge supplies of baleen they could elicit there from bowhead whales. Baleen is a flexible material found in the mouths of most whales that was used to make umbrellas, corset stays, fishing rods, and knitting needles, among other things.

The hunt for whales was, obviously, a very dangerous profession. Journeys often lasted as long as four years, and boredom, sickness, and death were accepted hazards of the job. Because of the harsh Arctic conditions, these whalers faced a set of perils unknown to those who went before them. The job of lookout was a particularly unpleasant one. There was little or no shelter from the elements in the crow's nest, which was situated 100 feet or more above the deck. Visibility, which was from eight to 12 miles in the Pacific ocean, was rarely more than six miles in the foggy Arctic, and often much less. Watches were for two hours at a time, and injury from falls or frostbite was common.

Today many species of whales are endangered or threatened, including the bowhead and the sperm whale. Only the Pacific Blue whale has increased inpopulation enough to be removed from the endangered list. Since 1946 the International Whaling Commission (IWC) has sought to limit, but not ban, commercial whaling. The IWC has no power to punish nations that exceed the limits that they set forth. Most nations have agreed to a total ban on commercial whaling, but in 1993 Norway and Japan lifted their bans.

Edie Freedman designed this cover. The cover image is adapted from a 19th-century engraving from the Bettman Archives. The cover layout was produced with Quark XPress 3.3 using the ITC Garamond font.

The inside formats were designed by Edie Freedman and implemented in sqtroff by Lenny Muellner. The text and heading fonts are ITC Garamond Light and Garamond Book. The illustrations that appear in the book were created in Aldus Freehand by Chris Reilley, and the screenshots were processed in Adobe PhotoShop using Photomatic. This colophon was written by Clairemarie Fisher O'Leary. Special thanks to Janet Hamilton of the Museum of Science in Boston for her help.

INTERNET

Books from O'Reilly & Associates, Inc.

FALL/WINTER 1994-95

The Whole Internet User's Guide & Catalog

By Ed Krol
2nd Edition April 1994
574 pages, ISBN 1-56592-063-5

The best book about the Internet just got better! This is the second edition of our comprehensive—and bestselling—introduction to the Internet, the international network that includes virtually every major computer site in the world. In addition to email, file transfer, remote login, and network news, this book pays special attention to some new tools for helping you find information. Useful to beginners and veterans alike, this book will help you explore what's possible on the Net. Also includes a pull-out quick-reference card.

"An ongoing classic."
—*Rochester Business Journal*

"The book against which all subsequent Internet guides are measured, Krol's work has emerged as an indispensable reference to beginners and seasoned travelers alike as they venture out on the data highway."
—*Microtimes*

"*The Whole Internet User's Guide & Catalog* will probably become the Internet user's bible because it provides comprehensive, easy instructions for those who want to get the most from this valuable electronic tool."
—David J. Buerger, Editor, *Communications Week*

"Krol's work is comprehensive and lucid, an overview which presents network basics in clear and understandable language. I consider it essential."
—Paul Gilster, *Triad Business News*

!%@:: A Directory of Electronic Mail Addressing & Networks

By Donnalyn Frey & Rick Adams
4th Edition June 1994
662 pages, ISBN 1-56592-046-5

This is the only up-to-date directory that charts the networks that make up the Internet, provides contact names and addresses, and describes the services each network provides. It includes all of the major Internet-based networks, as well as various commercial networks such as CompuServe, Delphi, and America Online that are "gatewayed" to the Internet for transfer of electronic mail and other services. If you are someone who wants to connect to the Internet, or someone who already is connected but wants concise, up-to-date information on many of the world's networks, check out this book.

This is the fourth edition of this directory, now in a simplified format designed to allow more frequent updates.

"The book remains the bible of electronic messaging today. One could easily borrow the American Express slogan with the quip 'don't do messaging without it.' The book introduces you to electronic mail in all its many forms and flavors, tells you about the networks throughout the world...with an up-to-date summary of information on each, plus handy references such as all the world's subdomains. The husband-wife team authors are among the most knowledgeable people in the Internet world. This is one of those publications for which you just enter a lifetime subscription."
—Book Review, *ISOC News*

The Mosaic Handbooks

Mosaic is an important application that is becoming instrumental in the growth of the Internet. These books, one for Microsoft Windows, one for the X Window System, and one for the Macintosh, introduce you to Mosaic and its use in navigating and finding information on the World Wide Web. They show you how to use Mosaic to replace some of the traditional Internet functions like FTP, Gopher, Archie, Veronica, and WAIS. For more advanced users, the books describe how to add external viewers to Mosaic (allowing it to display many additional file types) and how to customize the Mosaic interface, such as screen elements, colors, and fonts. The Microsoft and Macintosh versions come with a copy of Mosaic on a floppy disk; the X Window version comes with a CD-ROM. All three books come with a subscription to The Global Network Navigator (GNN)™, the leading WWW-based information service on the Internet.

The Mosaic Handbook for Microsoft Windows

By Dale Dougherty & Richard Koman
1st Edition October 1994
234 pages (est.), ISBN 1-56592-094-5
(Foppy disk included)

The Mosaic Handbook for the X Window System

By Dale Dougherty, Richard Koman &
Paula Ferguson
1st Edition October 1994
220 pages (est.), ISBN 1-56592-095-3
(CD-ROM included)

The Mosaic Handbook for the Macintosh

By Dale Dougherty & Richard Koman
1st Edition October 1994
220 pages (est.), ISBN 1-56592-096-1
(Floppy disk included)

Internet In A Box

Produced by Spry, Inc.
Available late September 1994
UPC 799364 01100
(sold only in the US and Canada)

Internet In A Box™ is the first shrink-wrapped package to provide a total solution for PC users to get on the Internet. *Internet In A Box* provides instant connectivity, a multimedia Windows interface, a full suite of applications, and a complete online guide to the Internet. The box contains:

- Two ways to connect to the Internet: five-minute automated connection via SprintLink or manual connection to any PPP provider in the US and Canada.

- A subscription to the Global Network Navigator (GNN)™, an online interactive guide to the Internet.

- Software: The Air Series applications, including Mosaic, electronic mail, Usenet news reader, drag-and-drop file transfer, gopher, and telnet.

- Three books that clearly describe how to use these resources: a special edition of Ed Krol's bestselling *The Whole Internet User's Guide & Catalog*, a *Getting Started* guide, and an *Install* guide.

Connecting to the Internet

By Susan Estrada
1st Edition August 1993
188 pages, ISBN 1-56592-061-9

This book provides practical advice on how to get an Internet connection. It describes how to assess your needs to determine the kind of Internet service that is best for you and how to find a local access provider and evaluate the services they offer.

Knowing how to purchase the right kind of Internet access can help you save money and avoid a lot of frustration. This book is the fastest way for you to learn how to get on the Internet. Then you can begin exploring one of the world's most valuable resources.

"A much needed 'how to do it' for anyone interested in getting Internet connectivity and using it as part of their organization or enterprise. The sections are simple and straightforward.... If you want to know how to connect your organization, get this book."
—Book Review, *ISOC News*

Learning the UNIX Operating System

By Grace Todino, John Strang & Jerry Peek
3rd Edition August 1993
108 pages, ISBN 1-56592-060-0

If you are new to UNIX, this concise introduction will tell you just what you need to get started and no more. Why wade through a 600-page book when you can begin working productively in a matter of minutes? It's an ideal primer for Mac and PC users of the Internet who need to know a little bit about UNIX on the systems they visit.

This book is the most effective introduction to UNIX in print. The third edition has been updated and expanded to provide increased coverage of window systems and networking. It's a handy book for someone just starting with UNIX, as well as someone who encounters a UNIX system as a "visitor" via remote login over the Internet.

"If you have someone on your site who has never worked on a UNIX system and who needs a quick how-to, Nutshell® has the right booklet. *Learning the UNIX Operating System* can get a newcomer rolling in a single session. It covers logging in and out; files and directories; mail; pipes; filters; backgrounding; and a large number of other topics. It's clear, cheap, and can render a newcomer productive in a few hours."
—*;login*

Smileys

By David W. Sanderson
1st Edition March 1993
93 pages, ISBN 1-56592-041-4

From the people who put an armadillo on the cover of a system administrator book comes this collection of the computer underground hieroglyphs called "smileys." Originally inserted into email messages to denote "said with a cynical smile" :-), smileys now run rampant throughout the electronic mail culture.

"For a quick grin at an odd moment, this is a nice pocket book to carry around :-) If you keep this book near your terminal, you could express many heretofore hidden feelings in your email ;-) Then again, such things may be frowned upon at your company :-(No matter, this is a fun book to have around."
—Gregory M. Amov, *News & Review*

TCP/IP Network Administration

By Craig Hunt
1st Edition August 1992
502 pages, ISBN 0-937175-82-X

TCP/IP Network Administration is a complete guide to setting up and running a TCP/IP network for administrators of networks of systems or lone home systems that access the Internet. It starts with the fundamentals: what the protocols do and how they work, how to request a network address and a name (the forms needed are included in an appendix), and how to set up your network.

Beyond basic setup, the book discusses how to configure important network applications, including sendmail, the r* commands, and some simple setups for NIS and NFS. There are also chapters on troubleshooting and security. In addition, this book covers several important packages that are available from the Net (such as *gated*). Covers BSD and System V TCP/IP implementations.

"*TCP/IP Network Administration* provides a great service to network managers. Any network manager responsible for TCP/IP networking should keep a copy of this inexpensive reference nearby."
—*Network Computing*

Managing Internet Information Services

By Cricket Liu, Jerry Peek, Russ Jones, Bryan Buus & Adrian Nye
1st Edition Winter 1994/95 (est.)
400 pages (est.), ISBN 1-56592-062-7

This comprehensive guide describes how to set up information services to make them available over the Internet. Providing complete coverage of all popular services, it discusses why a company would want to offer Internet services and how to select which ones to provide. Most of the book describes how to set up email services and FTP, Gopher, and World Wide Web servers.

"*Managing Internet Information Services* has long been needed in the Internet community, as well as in many organizations with IP-based networks. Although many on the Internet are quite savvy when it comes to administering these types of tools, MIIS will allow a much larger community to join in and perhaps provide more diverse information. This book will be a welcome addition to my Internet shelf."
—Robert H'obbes' Zakon, MITRE Corporation

sendmail

By Bryan Costales, with Eric Allman & Neil Rickert
1st Edition November 1993
830 pages, ISBN 1-56592-056-2

Although sendmail is used on almost every UNIX system, it's one of the last great uncharted territories—and most difficult utilities to learn—in UNIX system administration. This book provides a complete sendmail tutorial, plus extensive reference material. It covers the BSD, UIUC IDA, and V8 versions of sendmail.

"The program and its rule description file, sendmail.cf, have long been regarded as the pit of coals that separated the mild Unix system administrators from the real fire walkers. Now, sendmail syntax, testing, hidden rules, and other mysteries are revealed. Costales, Allman, and Rickert are the indisputable authorities to do the text."
—Ben Smith, *Byte*

DNS and BIND

By Cricket Liu & Paul Albitz
1st Edition October 1992
418 pages, ISBN 1-56592-010-4

DNS and BIND contains all you need to know about the Internet's Domain Name System (DNS) and the Berkeley Internet Name Domain (BIND), its UNIX implementation. The Domain Name System is the Internet's "phone book"; it's a database that tracks important information (in particular, names and addresses) for every computer on the Internet. If you're a system administrator, this book will show you how to set up and maintain the DNS software on your network.

"At 380 pages it blows away easily any vendor supplied information, and because it has an extensive troubleshooting section (using nslookup) it should never be far from your desk— especially when things on your network start to go awry :-)"
—Ian Hoyle, BHP Research, Melbourne Laboratories

MH & xmh: E-mail for Users & Programmers

By Jerry Peek
2nd Edition September 1992
728 pages, ISBN 1-56592-027-9

Customizing your email environment can save time and make communicating more enjoyable. *MH & xmh: E-Mail for Users & Programmers* explains how to use, customize, and program with the MH electronic mail commands available on virtually any UNIX system. The handbook also covers *xmh*, an X Window System client that runs MH programs.

The second edition added a chapter on mhook, sections explaining under-appreciated small commands and features, and more examples showing how to use MH to handle common situations.

"The MH bible is irrefutably Jerry Peek's *MH & xmh: E-mail for Users & Programmers*. This book covers just about everything that is known about MH and *xmh* (the X Windows front end to MH), presented in a clear and easy-to-read format. I strongly recommend that anybody serious about MH get a copy."
—James Hamilton, *UnixWorld*

Practical UNIX Security

By Simson Garfinkel & Gene Spafford
1st Edition June 1991
512 pages, ISBN 0-937175-72-2

Practical UNIX Security tells system administrators how to make their UNIX system—either System V or BSD—as secure as it possibly can be without going to trusted system technology. The book describes UNIX concepts and how they enforce security, tells how to defend against and handle security breaches, and explains network security (including UUCP, NFS, Kerberos, and firewall machines) in detail. If you are a UNIX system administrator or user who deals with security, you need this book.

"Timely, accurate, written by recognized experts...covers every imaginable topic relating to Unix security. An excellent book and I recommend it as a valuable addition to any system administrator's or computer site manager's collection."
—Jon Wright, *Informatics*(Australia)

O'Reilly & Associates—
GLOBAL NETWORK NAVIGATOR

The Global Network Navigator (GNN)™ is a unique kind of information service that makes the Internet easy and enjoyable to use. We organize access to the vast information resources of the Internet so that you can find what you want. We also help you understand the Internet and the many ways you can explore it.

In GNN you'll find:

Navigating the Net with GNN

 The *Whole Internet Catalog* contains a descriptive listing of the most useful Net resources and services with live links to those resources.

 The *GNN Business Pages* are where you'll learn about companies who have established a presence on the Internet and use its worldwide reach to help educate consumers.

The *Internet Help Desk* helps folks who are new to the Net orient themselves and gets them started on the road to Internet exploration.

News

NetNews is a weekly publication that reports on the news of the Internet, with weekly feature articles that focus on Internet trends and special events. The Sports, Weather, and Comix Pages round out the news.

Special Interest Publications

Whether you're planning a trip or are just interested in reading about the journeys of others, you'll find that the *Travelers' Center* contains a rich collection of feature articles and ongoing columns about travel. In the *Travelers' Center*, you can link to many helpful and informative travel-related Internet resources.

The *Personal Finance Center* is the place to go for information about money management and investment on the Internet. Whether you're an old pro at playing the market or are thinking about investing for the first time, you'll read articles and discover Internet resources that will help you to think of the Internet as a personal finance information tool.

All in all, GNN helps you get more value for the time you spend on the Internet.

 The Best of the Web

The *O'Reilly Resource Center* was voted **"Best Commercial Site"** by users participating in "Best of the Web '94."

GNN received "Honorable Mention" for **"Best Overall Site," "Best Entertainment Service,"** and **"Most Important Service Concept."**

The *GNN NetNews* received "Honorable Mention" for **"Best Document Design."**

Subscribe Today

GNN is available over the Internet as a subscription service. To get complete information about subscribing to GNN, send email to **info@gnn.com**. If you have access to a World Wide Web browser such as Mosaic or Lynx, you can use the following URL to register online: http://gnn.com/

If you use a browser that does not support online forms, you can retrieve an email version of the registration form automatically by sending email to **form@gnn.com**. Fill this form out and send it back to us by email, and we will confirm your registration.

AUDIOTAPES

O'Reilly now offers audiotapes based on interviews with people who are making a profound impact in the world of the Internet. Here we give you a quick overview of what's available. For details on our audiotape collection, send email to **audio@ora.com**.

"Ever listen to one of those five-minute-long news pieces being broadcast on National Public Radio's 'All Things Considered' and wish they were doing an in-depth story on new technology? Well, your wishes are answered." —Byte

Global Network Operations

Carl Malamud interviews Brian Carpenter, Bernhard Stockman, Mike O'Dell & Geoff Huston
Duration: 2 hours, ISBN 1-56592-993-4

What does it take to actually run a network? In these four interviews, Carl Malamud explores some of the technical and operational issues faced by Internet service providers around the world.

Brian Carpenter is the director for networking at CERN, the high-energy physics laboratory in Geneva, Switzerland. Physicists are some of the world's most active Internet users, and its global user base makes CERN one of the world's most network-intensive sites. Carpenter discusses how he deals with issues such as the OSI and DECnet Phase V protocols and his views on the future of the Internet.

Bernhard Stockman is one of the founders and the technical manager of the European Backbone (EBONE). EBONE has proven to be the first effective transit backbone for Europe and has been a leader in the deployment of CIDR, BGP-4, and other key technologies.

Mike O'Dell is vice president of research at UUNET Technologies. O'Dell has a long record of involvement in data communications, ranging from his service as a telco lab employee, an engineer on several key projects, and a member of the USENIX board to now helping define new services for one of the largest commercial IP service providers.

Geoff Huston is the director of the Australian Academic Research Network (AARNET). AARNET is known as one of the most progressive regional networks, rapidly adopting new services for its users. Huston talks about how networking in Australia has flourished despite astronomically high rates for long-distance lines.

The Future of the Internet Protocol

Carl Malamud interviews Steve Deering, Bob Braden, Christian Huitema, Bob Hinden, Peter Ford, Steve Casner, Bernhard Stockman & Noel Chiappa
Duration: 4 hours, ISBN 1-56592-996-9

The explosion of interest in the Internet is stressing what was originally designed as a research and education network. The sheer number of users is requiring new strategies for Internet address allocation; multimedia applications are requiring greater bandwidth and strategies such as "resource reservation" to provide synchronous end-to-end service.

In this series of eight interviews, Carl Malamud talks to some of the researchers who are working to define how the underlying technology of the Internet will need to evolve in order to meet the demands of the next five to ten years.

Give these tapes a try if you're intrigued by such topics as Internet "multicasting" of audio and video, or think your job might one day depend on understanding some of the following buzzwords:

- IPNG (Internet Protocol Next Generation)
- SIP (Simple Internet Protocol)
- TUBA (TCP and UDP with Big Addresses)
- CLNP (Connectionless Network Protocol)
- CIDR (Classless Inter-Domain Routing)

or if you are just interested in getting to know more about the people who are shaping the future.

Mobile IP Networking

Carl Malamud interviews Phil Karn & Jun Murai
Released Spring 1994
Duration: 1 hour, ISBN 1-56592-994-2

Phil Karn is the father of the KA9Q publicly available implementation of TCP/IP for DOS (which has also been used as the basis for the software in many commercial Internet routers). KA9Q was originally developed to allow "packet radio," that is, TCP/IP over ham radio bands. Phil's current research focus is on commercial applications of wireless data communications.

Jun Murai is one of the most distinguished researchers in the Internet community. Murai is a professor at Keio University and the founder of the Japanese WIDE Internet. Murai talks about his research projects, which range from satellite-based IP multicasting to a massive testbed for mobile computing at the Fujisawa campus of Keio University.

Networked Information and Online Libraries

Carl Malamud interviews Peter Deutsch & Cliff Lynch
Released September 1993
Duration: 1 hour, ISBN 1-56592-998-5

Peter Deutsch, president of Bunyip Information Services, was one of the co-developers of Archie. In this interview Peter talks about his philosophy for services and compares Archie to X.500. He also talks about what kind of standards we need for networked information retrieval.

Cliff Lynch is currently the director of library automation for the University of California. He discusses issues behind online publishing, such as SGML and the democratization of publishing on the Internet.

European Networking

Carl Malamud interviews Glenn Kowack & Rob Blokzijl
Released September 1993
Duration: 1 hour, ISBN 1-56592-999-3

Glenn Kowack is chief executive of EUnet, the network that's bringing the Internet to the people of Europe. Glenn talks about EUnet's populist business model and the politics of European networking.

Rob Blokzijl is the network manager for NIKHEF, the Dutch Institute of High Energy Physics. Rob talks about RIPE, the IP user's group for Europe, and the nuts and bolts of European network coordination.

Security and Networks

Carl Malamud interviews Jeff Schiller & John Romkey
Released September 1993
Duration: 1 hour, ISBN 1-56592-997-7

Jeff Schiller is the manager of MIT's campus network and is one of the Internet's leading security experts. Here, he talks about Privacy Enhanced Mail (PEM), the difficulty of policing the Internet, and whether horses or computers are more useful to criminals.

John Romkey has been a long-time TCP/IP developer and was recently named to the Internet Architecture Board. In this wide-ranging interview, John talks about the famous "ToasterNet" demo at InterOp, what kind of Internet security he'd like to see put in place, and what Internet applications of the future might look like.

John Perry Barlow
Notable Speeches of the Information Age

USENIX Conference Keynote Address
San Francisco, CA; January 17, 1994
Duration: 1.5 hours, ISBN 1-56592-992-6

John Perry Barlow—retired Wyoming cattle rancher, a lyricist for the Grateful Dead since 1971— holds a degree in comparative religion from Wesleyan University. He also happens to be a recognized authority on computer security, virtual reality, digitized intellectual property, and the social and legal conditions arising in the global network of computers.

In 1990 Barlow co-founded the Electronic Frontier Foundation with Mitch Kapor and currently serves as chair of its executive committee. He writes and lectures on subjects relating to digital technology and society and is a contributing editor to *Communications of the ACM, NeXTWorld, Microtimes, Mondo 2000, Wired*, and other publications.

In his keynote address to the Winter 1994 USENIX Conference, Barlow talks of recent developments in the national information infrastructure, telecommunications regulation, cryptography, globalization of the Internet, intellectual property, and the settlement of Cyberspace. The talk explores the premise that "architecture is politics": that the technology adopted for the coming "information superhighway" will help to determine what is carried on it, and that if the electronic frontier of the Internet is not to be replaced by electronic strip malls, we need to make sure that our technological choices favor bi-directional communication and open platforms.

Side A contains the keynote;
Side B contains a question and answer period.

O'Reilly on the Net—
ONLINE PROGRAM GUIDE

O'Reilly & Associates offers extensive information through our online resources. If you've got Internet access, we invite you to come and explore our little neck-of-the-woods.

Online Resource Center

Most comprehensive among our online offerings is the O'Reilly Resource Center. Here, you'll find detailed information and descriptions on all O'Reilly products: titles, prices, tables of contents, indexes, author bios, CD-ROM directory listings, reviews...you can even view images of the products themselves. We also supply helpful ordering information: how to contact us, how to order online, distributors and bookstores around the world, discounts, upgrades, etc. In addition, we provide informative literature in the field, featuring articles, interviews, bibliographies, and columns that help you stay informed and abreast.

To access ORA's Online Resource Center:

Point your Web browser (e.g., `mosaic` or `lynx`) to:

`http://gnn.com/ora/`

For the plaintext version, `telnet` or `gopher` to:

`gopher.ora.com`

Ora-news

An easy way to stay informed of the latest projects and products from O'Reilly & Associates is to subscribe to "ora-news," our electronic news service. Subscribers receive email as soon as the information breaks.

To subscribe to "ora-news":

Send email to:
listproc@online.ora.com

and put the following information on the first line of your message (not in "Subject"):
subscribe ora-news "your name" **of** "your company"

For example:
subscribe ora-news Jim Dandy of Mighty Fine Enterprises

FTP

The example files and programs in many of our books are available electronically via FTP.

To obtain example files and programs from O'Reilly texts:

`ftp` to:

`ftp.uu.net`
`cd published/oreilly`

or
`ftp.ora.com`

Email

Many other helpful customer services are provided via email. Here's a few of the most popular and useful.

Useful email addresses

nuts@ora.com
　　For general questions and information.

bookquestions@ora.com
　　For technical questions, or corrections, concerning
　　book contents.

order@ora.com
　　To order books online and for ordering questions.

catalog@ora.com
　　To receive a free copy of our magazine/catalog, "ora.com"
　　(please include a snailmail address).

Snailmail and phones

O'Reilly & Associates, Inc.
103A Morris Street, Sebastopol, CA 95472
Inquiries: **707-829-0515, 800-998-9938**
Credit card orders: **800-889-8969**
FAX: **707-829-0104**

O'Reilly & Associates—
LISTING OF TITLES

INTERNET

!%@:: A Directory of Electronic Mail
    Addressing & Networks
Connecting to the Internet: An O'Reilly Buyer's Guide
Internet In A Box
MH & xmh: E-mail for Users & Programmers
The Mosaic Handbook for Microsoft Windows
The Mosaic Handbook for the Macintosh
The Mosaic Handbook for the X Window System
Smileys
The Whole Internet User's Guide & Catalog

SYSTEM ADMINISTRATION

Computer Security Basics
DNS and BIND
Essential System Administration
Linux Network Administrator's Guide (Fall 94 est.)
Managing Internet Information Services (Fall 94 est.)
Managing NFS and NIS
Managing UUCP and Usenet
sendmail
Practical UNIX Security
PGP: Pretty Good Privacy (Winter 94/95 est.)
System Performance Tuning
TCP/IP Network Administration
termcap & terminfo
X Window System Administrator's Guide: Volume 8
X Window System ,R6, Companion CD (Fall 94 est.)

USING UNIX AND X

BASICS

Learning GNU Emacs
Learning the Korn Shell
Learning the UNIX Operating System
Learning the vi Editor
SCO UNIX in a Nutshell
The USENET Handbook (Winter 94/95 est.)
Using UUCP and Usenet
UNIX in a Nutshell: System V Edition
The X Window System in a Nutshell
X Window System User's Guide: Volume 3
X Window System User's Guide, Motif Ed.: Vol. 3M
X User Tools (10/94 est.)

ADVANCED

Exploring Expect (Winter 94/95 est.)
The Frame Handbook (10/94 est.)
Making TeX Work
Learning Perl
Programming perl
sed & awk
UNIX Power Tools (with CD-ROM)

PROGRAMMING UNIX, C, AND MULTI-PLATFORM

FORTRAN/SCIENTIFIC COMPUTING

High Performance Computing
Migrating to Fortran 90
UNIX for FORTRAN Programmers

C PROGRAMMING LIBRARIES

Practical C Programming
POSIX Programmer's Guide
POSIX.4: Programming for the Real World
    (Fall 94 est.)
Programming with curses
Understanding and Using COFF
Using C on the UNIX System

C PROGRAMMING TOOLS

Checking C Programs with lint
lex & yacc
Managing Projects with make
Power Programming with RPC
Software Portability with imake

MULTI-PLATFORM PROGRAMMING

Encyclopedia of Graphics File Formats
Distributing Applications Across DCE and
    Windows NT
Guide to Writing DCE Applications
Multi-Platform Code Management
Understanding DCE
Understanding Japanese Information Processing
ORACLE Performance Tuning

BERKELEY 4.4 SOFTWARE DISTRIBUTION

4.4BSD System Manager's Manual
4.4BSD User's Reference Manual
4.4BSD User's Supplementary Documents
4.4BSD Programmer's Reference Manual
4.4BSD Programmer's Supplementary Documents
4.4BSD-Lite CD Companion
4.4BSD-Lite CD Companion: International Version

X PROGRAMMING

Motif Programming Manual: Volume 6A
Motif Reference Manual: Volume 6B
Motif Tools
PEXlib Programming Manual
PEXlib Reference Manual
PHIGS Programming Manual (soft or hard cover)
PHIGS Reference Manual
Programmer's Supplement for R6 (Winter 94/95 est.)
Xlib Programming Manual: Volume 1
Xlib Reference Manual: Volume 2
X Protocol Reference Manual, R5: Volume 0
X Protocol Reference Manual, R6: Volume 0 (11/94 est.)
X Toolkit Intrinsics Programming Manual: Vol. 4
X Toolkit Intrinsics Programming Manual,
    Motif Edition: Volume 4M
X Toolkit Intrinsics Reference Manual: Volume 5
XView Programming Manual: Volume 7A
XView Reference Manual: Volume 7B

THE X RESOURCE

A QUARTERLY WORKING JOURNAL FOR X PROGRAMMERS

The X Resource: Issues 0 through 12
    (Issue 12 available 10/94)

BUSINESS/CAREER

Building a Successful Software Business
Love Your Job!

TRAVEL

Travelers' Tales Thailand
Travelers' Tales Mexico
Travelers' Tales India (Winter 94/95 est.)

AUDIOTAPES

INTERNET TALK RADIO'S "GEEK OF THE WEEK" INTERVIEWS

The Future of the Internet Protocol, 4 hours
Global Network Operations, 2 hours
Mobile IP Networking, 1 hour
Networked Information and
    Online Libraries, 1 hour
Security and Networks, 1 hour
European Networking, 1 hour

NOTABLE SPEECHES OF THE INFORMATION AGE

John Perry Barlow, 1.5 hours

O'Reilly & Associates—
INTERNATIONAL DISTRIBUTORS

Customers outside North America can now order O'Reilly & Associates books through the following distributors. They offer our international customers faster order processing, more bookstores, increased representation at tradeshows worldwide, and the high quality, responsive service our customers have come to expect.

EUROPE, MIDDLE EAST, AND AFRICA

(except Germany, Switzerland, and Austria)

INQUIRIES

International Thomson Publishing Europe
Berkshire House
168-173 High Holborn
London WC1V 7AA
United Kingdom
Telephone: 44-71-497-1422
Fax: 44-71-497-1426
Email: danni.dolbear@itpuk.co.uk

ORDERS

International Thomson Publishing Services, Ltd.
Cheriton House, North Way
Andover, Hampshire SP10 5BE
United Kingdom
Telephone: 44-264-342-832 (UK orders)
Telephone: 44-264-342-806 (outside UK)
Fax: 44-264-364418 (UK orders)
Fax: 44-264-342761 (outside UK)

GERMANY, SWITZERLAND, AND AUSTRIA

International Thomson Publishing GmbH
O'Reilly-International Thomson Verlag
Attn: Mr. G. Miske
Königswinterer Strasse 418
53227 Bonn
Germany
Telephone: 49-228-970240
Fax: 49-228-441342
Email: ora_de@ora.com

THE AMERICAS, JAPAN, AND OCEANIA

O'Reilly & Associates, Inc.
103A Morris Street
Sebastopol, CA 95472 U.S.A.
Telephone: 707-829-0515
Telephone: 800-998-9938 (U.S. & Canada)
Fax: 707-829-0104
Email: order@ora.com

ASIA

(except Japan)

INQUIRIES

International Thomson Publishing Asia
221 Henderson Road
#05 10 Henderson Building
Singapore 0315
Telephone: 65-272-6496
Fax: 65-272-6498

ORDERS

Telephone: 65-268-7867
Fax: 65-268-6727

AUSTRALIA

WoodsLane Pty. Ltd.
Unit 8, 101 Darley Street (P.O. Box 935)
Mona Vale NSW 2103
Australia
Telephone: 61-2-9795944
Fax: 61-2-9973348

NEW ZEALAND

WoodsLane New Zealand Ltd.
21 Cooks Street (P.O. Box 575)
Wanganui, New Zealand
Telephone: 64-6-3476543
Fax: 64-6-3454840
Email: woods@tmx.mhs.oz.au

O'Reilly & Associates, Inc.
End-User License Agreement

NOTICE! CAREFULLY READ ALL OF THE TERMS AND CONDITIONS OF THIS AGREEMENT PRIOR TO OPENING THIS PACKAGE. REMOVING THE DISK FROM ITS PLASTIC CONTAINER INDICATES YOUR ACCEPTANCE OF THE FOLLOWING TERMS AND CONDITIONS. IF YOU DO NOT AGREE TO THESE TERMS AND CONDITIONS, RETURN THE UNOPENED DISK PACKAGE AND ANY OTHER COMPONENTS OF THIS PRODUCT TO O'REILLY & ASSOCIATES, INC. ("O'REILLY") FOR A FULL REFUND. NO REFUND WILL BE GIVEN IF THIS PACKAGE HAS BEEN OPENED OR COMPONENTS OF THE PRODUCT ARE MISSING.

1. **License:** This License Agreement (the "Agreement") permits you to use one copy of the computer program contained on the disk in object code form only (the "Program") on any single computer for your own internal business purposes (the "License"). If you have multiple Licenses for multiple copies of the Program, then the number of copies of the Program in use must never exceed the number of Licenses held; if the anticipated number of users of the Program will exceed the number of Licenses held, then you must have in place a reasonable mechanism or procedure to ensure that the number of persons using the Program concurrently does not exceed the number of Licenses held. For purposes of this Agreement, the Program is "in use" when it is loaded into temporary memory (e.g., RAM) or installed into the permanent memory (e.g., hard disk, CD-ROM, or any other storage device) of any computer.

2. **Copying of Program:** You may make one copy of the Program solely for back-up or archival purposes provided that such copy contains the notices described in paragraph 4 below. Any other copying of the Program or the accompanying documentation is in violation of this Agreement and applicable intellectual property laws. You may not decompile, disassemble or otherwise reverse-engineer the Program.

3. **Transfer of Program:** The Program may not be transferred, assigned, or sublicensed to any third party.

4. **Copyright:** The Program and the accompanying documentation is protected by United Sates and international copyright laws and international trade provisions. You may not remove, obscure, or alter any notice of patent, copyright, trademark, trade secret or other proprietary right contained in the Program or the accompanying documentation. The licensee acknowledges that it has no right, title, or interest in or to the Program or the accompanying documentation including without limitation, patent, copyright, trademark, trade secret or any other proprietary right, except for the License specifically granted herein.

5. **Term:** The License granted hereunder shall be effective until terminated. The License shall terminate automatically should you violate any part of this agreement; in the event of such termination you will no longer be entitled to use the Program and must destroy all copies of the Program or return them to O'Reilly. You may also elect to terminate this Agreement and the License by destroying all copies of the Program or returning such copies to O'Reilly.

6. **Limited Warranty; Disclaimer and Limitation of Liability:** THE PROGRAM IS BEING PROVIDED "AS IS" WITHOUT WARRANTY OF ANY KIND AND O'REILLY HEREBY DISCLAIMS ALL WARRANTIES, WHETHER EXPRESS OR IMPLIED, ORAL OR WRITTEN, WITH RESPECT TO THE PROGRAM INCLUDING WITHOUT LIMITATION, IMPLIED WARRANTIES OF MERCHANTABILITY OR FITNESS FOR ANY PARTICULAR PURPOSE. IN NO EVENT SHALL O'REILLY BE LIABLE FOR INDIRECT OR CONSEQUENTIAL DAMAGES, INCLUDING WITHOUT LIMITATION, LOSS OF INCOME OR PROFITS; NOR SHALL O'REILLY'S LIABILITY IN ANY CASE EXCEED THE AMOUNT PAID FOR THE PROGRAM LICENSE. THIS LIMITED WARRANTY GIVES YOU SPECIFIC LEGAL RIGHTS; YOU MAY HAVE OTHERS WHICH VARY FROM STATE TO STATE.

7. **General:** This agreement constitutes the entire Agreement between you and O'Reilly and supercedes any prior written or oral agreements concerning the Program, the accompanying documentation, or any other contents of the product package. This Agreement may not be modified except by a writing signed by both parties. O'Reilly shall not be bound by any provision of any purchase order, receipt, acceptance, confirmation, correspondence or other similar document unless O'Reilly specifically indicates its acceptance in writing. This Agreement shall be governed by and construed in accordance with the laws of the State of California.

8. **U.S. Government Restricted Rights:** Use, duplication or disclosure of the Program by any unit or agency of the United States Government (the "Government") is subject to the restrictions set forth in FAR 52.227-19 (c) (2), the Rights in Technical Data and Computer Software clause of DFARS 252.227-7013 (c) (1) (ii), and any similar or successor clauses in the FAR, DFARS, or the DoD or NASA FAR Supplement, whichever are applicable. In addition to the foregoing, the Government agrees to be bound and abide by the terms and conditions set forth in this Agreement. All rights reserved under the copyright laws of the United States. Contractor/manufacturer is O'Reilly & Associates, Inc., 103A Morris Street, Sebastopol, CA 95472.

3419